Copyright © 2014 by Lani Sharp
All rights reserved. This book or any portion thereof
may not be reproduced or used in any manner whatsoever
without the express written permission of the publisher
except for the use of brief quotations in a book review.

Printed in Australia

First Printing, 2014

ISBN 9780992520229

White Light Publishing House
10 Adina Ct
Kurunjang VIC, Australia 3337

www.whitelightpublishingau.com

ABOUT THE AUTHOR

☾ ★ ☽

Lani Sharp is a Natural Born Rebel who just also happens to be an Aquarian, who shunned 'conventional' astrology courses to pursue her own path in the wondrous, inspiring and ever-evolving field of cosmic forces and stellar influences. After failing to find a course or tutor that suited her needs, Lani set out on her own starry adventure across the skies, partly to discover her own 'truths' about this ancient system, but mostly to prove that one can achieve absolutely anything, including and above all, their dream careers (or living), if they put their hearts and souls into it. A self-taught astrologer who takes the spiritual and psychological approach to this much-loved popular art, she has been studying and effectively practising astrology since she was eight years old. When she is not writing about, channelling, practising or teaching astrology, she can be found living her dream life alternating somewhere between her tropical home in Australia's stunning North and her second home in Victoria's beautiful Dandenong Ranges, enjoying tea parties with her highly imaginative Cancerian daughter, Allira, and her gnome and fairy friends (who are Lani's friends), crystal-wishing, day-dreaming, believing in gnomes, pixies, magic and miracles, honing her magickal witchcraft skills, Moon-gazing, Sun-worshipping, Venus-channelling, Jupiter-drawing, assisting others to find and follow their spiritual paths ... or of course walking across rainbows!

ACKNOWLEDGEMENTS, CREDITS & GRATITUDE BLESSINGS

I would love to thank the following people and entities for their amazing contributions, interest, support and faith in me as I wrote the manuscripts for each of the twelve astrological Sun signs. Firstly, my wonderful partner, Travis, for his patience (no mean feat for a Gemini!), for supporting me every step of the way, and for his acceptance of my 'mad scientist' Aquarian mindset by never trying to break down the invisible 'laboratory' walls I built around myself while writing the books. I would also like to extend my enormous gratitude to the following: Allira, my little Cancerian 'crab' daughter, who also had to tolerate and operate within the bounds of her nutty professor mother's antics and focus throughout the writing of the books. Also, a big thanks to my Mum, Sandra, and my stepdad, Barry, for their unending support, love, advice, daily Skype conversations, acceptance of our geographical distance, and above all, their inner knowing that everything always comes together in the end. Thank you to Nicola, my wonderful Facebook friend, for recommending White Light Publishing House, and of course to White Light Publishing House themselves, for putting their faith (and patience) in my project from the very beginning - and an even bigger thank you to the wonderful people behind the company for publishing my work, Christie and Jess! Gratitude also goes out to the producers of my favourite brand of Nature's Cuppa Earl Grey tea, Eatrite, for their exceptional product, which assisted me through many late-night writing sessions, early morning editing and the mid-afternoon ebbs and flows of inspired ideas. I didn't even need to drink it sometimes, even just the exquisite bergamot fragrance was enough to carry me that little bit higher above myself; in a word (or two), simply divine. I have saved my final thank you for The Universe, who always delivers to me exactly what I have asked for, without exception. The Universe is my ultimate higher power, my guiding light, my powerful driving force, my eternal friend, my inner motivator, my sympathetic listener, my inspirational teacher, and the fulfiller of all my dreams, including this one, having my very first book published, a long-held dream that stretches way back through the years to my days of being a mini dreamer, inquisitor and stargazer. The Universe has always believed in me, but perhaps more importantly, I have always believed in *IT*.

So to all of the above, thank you, thank you, thank you.

INSPIRED BY ALL THE SIGNS

Aries imparted courage and boldness
And helped me dance away the pain
Taurus gave me hugs and comfort
And shelter from the rain
Gemini provided me with laughter
And taught me again how to have fun
Cancer nurtured and sustained me
By reflecting back my Sun
Leo reminded me there was joy
From within myself and above
Virgo awakened my healthy glow
By teaching me how to love
Libra gave me gentle hugs
And judged me not for a thing
Scorpio lent me some of his power
And took away the sting
Sagittarius showered me with gifts
Of words so wise and true
As Capricorn led the way up the mountain
My resolve and strength grew
Aquarius gave me the gift of friendship
And carried me as his brother
And Pisces swam with me to the depths
With a compassion like no other.

THE UNIVERSE

♥

Within you resides the merging of the Sun and the Moon, the dance of the constellations, the vibrations of the planets, and the vast microcosm and macrocosm of the entire Universe.

Uni means 'one' and Verse means 'song'; therefore, the word Universe literally means 'One Song'. How will you dance to your 'One Song'?

> *"There was a star danced, and under that I was born"*
>
> William Shakespeare

POWER ASTROLOGY

By Lani Sharp

AQUARIUS

Tapping into the Powers of Your Sun Sign for Greater Luck, Happiness, Health, Abundance & Love

"That which is above is like to that which is below, and that which is below is like to that which is above, to accomplish the miracles of one thing ... the Father thereof is the Sun, the mother the Moon."

The Emerald Tablet, Hermes Trismegistus, circa 3000 BC

★ ASTROLOGY ★

Astrology: "Divination through the correlation of earthly events with celestial patterns"

'Real Magic', I. Bonewits, 1971

The word astrology is derived from the Greek word astron, meaning 'star' and logos which means 'word'. Astrology, therefore, literally means language of the stars. It is based on the ancient law known as 'As Above, So Below', otherwise known as the Law of the Macrocosm and Microcosm. The Macrocosm is the Universe, symbolised by the sky, the starry dome that we can see from the Earth; the Microcosm is us - humans, and all other life on Earth. 'As Above, So Below' is a well-known and deeply impressing maxim of Hermetic origin, inscribed upon the 'Emerald Tablet' in cryptic wording by Hermes Trismegistus around 5,000 years ago. These four powerful words are adopted by astrologers and believers in magic to explain, in very succinct wording, the meaning behind the art and science of celestial influences upon our earthly affairs.

Astrology and many other magical studies, propose that we are not separate from the Universe, we are part of it. The Sun, Moon and planets all follow exact patterns of movement and their motions can be measured precisely by astronomers. The basic idea of astrology is that all individual parts of the

Universe, from plants to animals, cooperate with each other and work together in harmony.

Astrology is a science which has spanned many centuries and still remains extraordinarily popular, and its truths have the potential to speak to and *through* all of us. Long before today's interest in it, men of great vision such as Ptolemy, Hippocrates, Plato, Galileo, Jefferson, Franklin, Newton, Columbus and Jung respected its inherent truths, mythology and eternal knowledge. Furthermore, astrology predates many other 'sciences' - for out of it grew religion, medicine and astronomy, not the other way around.

The discipline of astrology is a study of the interlocking and interrelated forces of the twelve zodiacal forces, or constellations, that grace the skies above, as they pour their energies into the earthly kingdoms below. As these various energies circulate throughout the etheric realm of our solar system, these zodiacal entities and archetypes imprint their vibrational frequencies and harmonic resonances upon our bodies, minds, souls and spirits.

Since the earliest period of the history of man people studied the starry vaults of the heavens and conceived that their presence, movements and positions endowed us with divine influence. There is much evidence that positions and movements of the planets as seen from Earth at the time of birth are linked to personality characteristics of individuals.

Human energy and emotional cycles are governed by the forces and networks of magnetic impulses from all the planets. Of all the heavenly bodies, the Moon's effects and power are the most marked and visible due to its close proximity to Earth. But the Sun, Venus, Mars, Mercury, Jupiter, Saturn, Uranus, Neptune and Pluto exercise their influences just as surely. In fact, scientists are aware that plants and animals are affected by natural cycles which are governed by forces such as fluctuations in barometric pressure, the gravitational field and electricity in the air. These earthly dynamics are originally triggered by magnetic vibrations from the atmosphere, or outer space, from where the planets send forth their unseen waves. No living organism or mineral on Earth escapes these immense influences.

The geomagnetic field seems to affect life on earth in certain observed ways, and these influences appear to correlate with planetary positions. It has been suggested that the fluctuations of the Earth's magnetic field are picked up by the nervous system of the in utero infant, which acts like an antenna, and these synchronise the internal biological clocks of the foetus which control the moment of birth. The foetal magnetic antenna, therefore are sensitive enough to sense these planetary vibrations and fields, and through a combination of inherited genetics and the positions of the planets at birth, they are imprinted with certain basic inherited and 'absorbed' personality characteristics.

Carl Jung, the Swiss psychiatrist and psychological theorist, suggested that the inherent disposition of the individual is present at birth, and is reflected in the patterns of his or her natal chart. Further, he theorised that there is a 'priori factor' in all human activities, namely the inborn, preconscious and unconscious individual structure of the psyche. The preconscious psyche, for example that of a newborn baby, is not simply an empty vessel into which practically anything can be poured, but rather it is this preconscious psyche that gives us the free will to become what we are instead of what others or our environment makes us. The child is not merely a receptacle for the psychic life of those around him or her, albeit sensitive and susceptible to the surrounding unconscious forces in childhood; he/she also brings something of his own to his experience of them.

Further, Dr Harold S. Burr, who was a Professor of Anatomy at the Yale University School of Medicine, and author of *The Nature of Man and the Meaning of Existence* (1962), asserted that there is order in the universe, unity in the organism and man is endowed with a soul. He stated that a complex magnetic field not only establishes the pattern of the human brain at birth, but continues to regulate and control it through life, and that the human central nervous system is a superb receptor of electro-magnetic energies, the finest in nature. He contended that the electro-dynamic fields of all living things, which may be measured and mapped with standard voltmeters, mould and control each organism's development, health and mood, naming these fields 'fields of life'.

It can therefore be suggested that astrological and planetary influences endow us with the majority of our characteristics at birth, characteristics bestowed upon us according to our Sun sign and other planetary forces. Other parts of the chart are also highly significant and need to be integrated for a 'whole' picture to form, however the Sun sign is an excellent starting point.

Before the temple of the Oracle at Delphi, the ancient Greeks imparted a special piece of advice that was carved onto one of the portals: "Know Thyself." These two powerful words are easy enough to understand, but much more difficult to apply. Throughout life's inner and outer journey, astrology can provide us with an inner navigational system by which we can be guided towards our highest potential, and closer towards the eternal quest of 'knowing thyself'. It provides the hope that this higher spiritual plane exists and that if we can 'read' and therefore be guided by the unique inner blueprint that our individual birth chart has stamped upon us at the moment we take our very first breath, indeed we can reach this higher spiritual plane and realise our innate potential.

"We were born at a given moment, in a given place, and like vintage years of wine, we have the qualities of the year and of the season in which we are born" - *Carl Jung*

Always remember that astrology is not fatalistic.

The stars may incline, but they do not compel. Astrology simply provides us with an inner guide for our journey through life and the finding of our true selves - and what we do with it is entirely up to us.

Good luck on your journey!

THE SUN

Earth's Luminary: Our Brightest Shining Star

Our Centre, Core Self, Identity & Inner Guiding Light

The Sun is our centre, source, ego strength, essence, power, life force, will, vitality, creative expression, purpose, life's direction, our sense of identity, and what we really *are*.

It is the core of our individuality, our inner guiding light. It is externalising, and represents totality, infinity, eternity, the striving and ultimate reaching of personal destiny, and 'completion' in all areas. It is the creative energising giver of life and the 'father' of the zodiac. It endows us with our inherent creative potential and personal identity - our urge to *create* and to *be*. The Sun is our core self, conscious purpose, our sense of creating something out of our own being. It is the integrated personality and represents the *present*, our greatest Gift. The Sun rules the heart and is thus symbolically the centre of self.

Indeed, the Sun *is* the heart and the most commanding presence in our birth chart; the luminary Ruler who governs our essential self and above all, wants to shine, be noticed and be appreciated.

★ KEY WORDS ★

Identity, core self, spirit, life force, power, creativity, higher self, the Father, ego, vitality, pride, individuality, leadership, majesty, will, expression, purpose, the journey, the path and the destiny.

THE SUN - WHAT IT REPRESENTS IN THE HUMAN PSYCHE & NATAL CHART

"The Sun is the most powerful of all the stellar bodies. It colours the personality so strongly that an amazingly accurate picture can be given of the individual who was born when it was exercising its power through the known and predicable influences of a certain astrological sign; these electromagnetic vibrations will continue to stamp that person with the characteristics of their Sun sign as they go through life."

Linda Goodman's Sun Signs (1970)

The Sun is our essence, our core self, conscious purpose and sense of identity, our creative potential, our spirit, the integrated personality that shines outward from within us. It is concerned with the present. It is our centre, source, power, life force, will, vitality, purpose, life's direction, what & who we *really* are.

The Sun represents our basic urge for self-expression. It is the 'solar energy cell' in a person's character, the Lord and giver of life, and symbolises the way in which an individual will shine out to the world. Our Sun is our personal identity and aspects to it from other components in the chart show the ease or otherwise of assuredness and confidence with which one will project and express one's individuality. The Sun sign will also show how an individual bounces back from setbacks and disappointments, one's resilience and their general outward expression of energy.

The Sun is the archetype of the Father and represents the primary masculine principle in the natal chart. It indicates how we express and experience our masculine side, our conscious self, how we express ourselves creatively, personal potential, individuality, self-expression and personal power. It has to do with courage, power, generosity, creativity, vitality, self-confidence, nobility, self-worth, dignity and strength of will. It symbolises authority and purpose, the ruler, and its potential is the peak of constructive maturity. It signifies self-sufficiency and abundance, containing enough energy to radiate warmth and life to everything around it.

The sign in which one's Sun is posited, and its placement in the birth chart, strongly indicates the level and type of vitality available to the personality (the sign), and in which area of life this may be most strongly directed (the house).

The Sun in a natal chart is a powerful symbol because everything is filtered, at a conscious level, through it. It tells us what we need to do to feel fully alive, the type of engine 'driving' us, what we need to do to be authentic and to be fully functioning. Listening to the special message of one's Sun sign can provide one with direction, energy and life purpose.

The symbol for the Sun ☉ depicts a circle with a dot or 'seed' at its centre, from which the core self, power, creativity and the first sparks of life can spring. The circle around this 'seed' represents spirit, symbolising wholeness, eternity and the never-ending flow of energy.

While the Moon, the night sky's luminary, represents the *soul*, the Sun, the day sky's luminary, represents our *spirit*.

There is a reason your Sun sign is otherwise known as your Star Sign - it's because, quite simply, the Sun *is* a star; in fact, it's the largest, brightest, shiniest one in Earth's known visible Universe. This book is about your Sun sign and how you can become much larger, glow with far more brilliance and shine brighter than you ever dreamed possible. I wish you all the magic in the galaxy for your dreams to come true and your deepest wishes to become reality, through tapping into the amazing power and inherent potential of your Sun sign. So get set for a galactical ride through the lucky stars of your constellation - and may a shooting star cross the path in front of you as you go!

AQUARIUS THE WATER BEARER

"I pour the waters of knowledge forth onto a thirsty world"

★ Fixed Air, Masculine, Positive, Thinking ★

How Aquarius Emanates its Life Force / Energy

Originally, objectively, unconventionally, gregariously

Is Concerned With

★ Experimentation ★ Scientific thinking ★

★ Friendship ★ Brotherhood ★ Humanity ★

★ Kindness ★ Humaneness ★ Originality ★

★ Mystery, intrigues ★ Magic ★ Genius ★

★ Eccentricity ★ Independence ★ Freedom ★

★ Politics ★ Creative arts ★ Detachment ★

★ Electricity ★ Magnetism ★ Idealism ★ Logic ★

★ Telecommunications ★ Intellect ★ Rationality ★

SPIRITUAL AQUARIUS

Your Archetypal Universal Qualities

The Humanitarian, Rebel, Reformer, Global One

What You Refuse

To be ordinary or conventional

What You Are an Authority On

Truth, originality, genius and futuristic thinking

The Main Senses Through Which You Experience Your Reality

Truth, freedom, independence, originality

How You Love

Loyally, with friendship

Positive Characteristics

★ Communicative ★ Thoughtful ★ Humane ★

★ Independence in thought and action ★

★ Inventive, innovative and original ★

★ Friendly ★ Intellectual ★ Faithful ★

★ Interest in others ★ Cooperative ★

★ Absence of ego and arrogance ★ Loyal ★

★ Scientific ★ Unique ★ Original ★

★ Forward-thinking and futuristic ★

Negative Characteristics

★ Unwilling to share ideas ★

★ Erratic ★ Tactless ★ Rebellious ★

★ Eccentric ★ Perverse ★ Opinionated ★

★ Unwilling to fight for beliefs ★ Contradictory ★

★ Cranky ★ Aloof ★ Distant ★ Contrary ★

★ Afraid of intimacy ★ Unpredictable ★

★ Voyeuristic curiosity about people ★

★ Uncertainty ★ Lack of confidence ★

To Bring Out Your Best

Travel to offbeat places and immerse yourself in cultures, study foreign languages and diverse subjects, share your scientific, genius, insightful thinking with others, buy high-tech gadgets, be your own boss, express your individuality and shine!

Spiritual Goal: *To shine brighter by unleashing your talents, to learn to commit and see that it ultimately leads to freedom, to be more discriminate in your social crusading and 'battles', and to develop greater self-confidence.*

AQUARIUS
20 January - 18 February

Fixed Air

Ruled by Uranus

"I KNOW"

Gemstones Amethyst, Garnet, Aquamarine

★

Detached, independent, freedom-seeking, charitable, intuitive, impersonal, free-spirited, scientific, eccentric, visionary, rebellious, unconventional, non-conforming, original, unaffectionate, honest, unpredictable, idealistic, distant, friendly, group-oriented, imaginative, erratic, futuristic, innovative, cranky, stubborn, progressive, perverse, aloof, intellectual, contrary, paradoxical

"'But I don't want to go among mad people", Alice remarked. "Oh, you can't help that", said the Cat. "We're all mad here." - *Alice in Wonderland*

AQUARIUS

♒

★ Original ★ Free-spirited ★ Idealistic ★

★ Inventive ★ Independent ★ Eccentric ★

★ Visionary ★ Humanitarian ★

Aquarius is the sign of the Water Bearer, a man who pours the water of knowledge from its urn to benefit all of mankind. Friendly, inventive, detached, future-oriented, unconventional, rebellious, eccentric, aloof, idealistic and humanitarian are Aquarius' most notable traits. Being an intellectual air sign, this is a thinking rather than feeling character, and possesses a scientific and forward-thinking mind which it often puts to use for the advantage of all to great effect. Group-oriented but impersonal, Aquarius is often hard to pin down due to its aloof, cool and contrary nature. The Water Bearer is a paradoxical sign, with a great love of humankind but an aversion to close personal relationships; it is also broad-minded and far-sighted but tends to hide its intuitive truths and prophecies (which almost always come true) under a veil of contradiction, and perversely rebelling for its own sake. Humanitarian and social causes are a big thing for the progressive Water Bearer's spirit, and it will always fight for the underdog and those it feels are treated unfairly. Aquarius is futuristic, unorthodox, honest and truth-seeking, with very little ego but much conviction invested in its many ideals. An independent lover, loyal friend and with a great need for personal freedom, Aquarius is the eleventh sign and the offbeat and rebellious social crusader of the zodiac, whose lack of personal warmth is more than made up for by its gregarious far-reaching nature, and charitable and inventive contributions to all its fellow terrestrial inhabitants.

QUOTES BY AQUARIANS

"To believe in the things you can see and touch is no belief at all; but to believe in the unseen is a triumph and a blessing" - Abraham Lincoln (12 Feb, 1809)

"It's a funny thing about life; if you refuse to accept anything but the best, you very often get it" - W. Somerset Maugham (25 Jan, 1874)

"Accomplishments have no colour" - Leontyne Price (10 Feb, 1927)

"Genius is only one per cent inspiration and ninety-nine per cent perspiration" - Thomas Alva Edison (11 Feb, 1847)

"A wise man will make more opportunities than he finds" - Francis Bacon (22 Jan, 1561)

"In charity there is no excess" - Francis Bacon

"A loving heart is the truest wisdom" - Charles Dickens (7 Feb, 1812)

"No one is useless in this world who eases the burden of it to anyone else" - Charles Dickens

"When you reach the end of your rope, tie a knot in it and hang on" - Franklin D. Roosevelt (30 Jan, 1882)

"To believe in the things you can see and touch is no belief at all; but to believe in the unseen is a triumph and a blessing" - Abraham Lincoln (12 Feb, 1809)

"Charity begins at home, and justice begins next door" - Charles Dickens

"In wilderness I sense the miracle of life, and behind it our scientific accomplishments fade to trivia" - Charles Lindbergh (4 Feb, 1902)

"Every moment of one's existence is growing into more or retreating into less. One is always living a little more or dying a little bit" - Norman Mailer (31 Jan, 1923)

"Real freedom lies in wildness, not in civilisation" - Charles Lindbergh

"Men are not prisoners of fate, but only prisoners of their own minds" - Franklin D. Roosevelt

"Life is like a landscape. You live in the midst of it but can describe it only from the vantage point of distance" - Charles Lindbergh

"Is it worse to be scared than to be bored, that is the question" - Gertrude Stein (3 Feb, 1874)

"I try to decorate my imagination as much as I can" - Franz Schubert (31 Jan, 1797)

"Man knows much more than he understands" - Alfred Adler (7 Feb 1870)

"Considering how dangerous everything is, nothing is really very frightening" - Gertrude Stein

"Your silence will not protect you" - Audre Lorde (18 Feb 1934)

"The only thing we have to fear is fear itself" - Franklin D. Roosevelt

"I've been rich and I've been poor. It's better to be rich" - Gertrude Stein

"You cannot teach a man anything; you can only teach him to discover it within himself" - Galileo Galilei (15 Feb, 1564)

"The biggest adventure you can take is to live the life of your dreams" - Oprah Winfrey (29 Jan, 1954)

AQUARIUS

KEY CONCEPTS

★ Loyalty to a cause, ideal or idea ★

★ Talkative, active mentality ★

★ Gregarious, humane and sociable ★

★ Intuitive and alert mind ★

★ Impersonal, cool, aloof ★

★ Lacks sympathy on an individual

or personal level ★

★ Zealous and fanatical ★

★ Conceives zany, impractical schemes ★

★ Strives for brotherhood ★

★ Can embrace and love all equally ★

SOME CORRESPONDENCES THAT ARE ASSOCIATED WITH AQUARIUS

Astrology, advanced thought, batteries, radio and television broadcasting, computers, reformers, researchers, cooperative societies, friendship clubs, altruism, hopes and wishes, invention, lightning, modern technology, nuclear physics, electricity, electronics, the new age, aeronautics, rebels, the space age, social circles, group activities, scientists, X-ray technicians, as well as anything which is avant garde, detached, erratic, unorthodox, nonconformist, unusual, quirky, rebellious, paradoxical and unpredictable. Take your pick and enjoy the ride!

THE AQUARIAN SYMBOL

The image of Aquarius is that of a Water Bearer pouring forth the waters of knowledge and consciousness. However, these flowing waters are often mistakenly linked with the Water element, leading many to consider Aquarius a Water sign, when it is in fact an Air sign. Furthermore, the glyph for Aquarius is two waves, one on top of the other, and this was the Egyptian hieroglyphic for water. With all the obvious references to liquid ('Aquarius' itself was derived from the Latin aqua = water), it is little wonder that Aquarius is often mistaken for a Water sign.

The meaning of Aquarius is intertwined with the concept of a divine substance which nourishes all life, this substance being variously described as the waters of life, or a life-giving liquid. The esoteric significance of its meaning and symbol relates to the fluids that the Man in the image distributes from his urn, in that they are actually the waters of consciousness, or knowledge, which are related to the mind (the Air element) that he is pouring from his vessel, and not related to 'pouring forth' of feelings or emotions (the Water element). This consciousness embraces the concept that all humans are brothers, a concept which can only be felt intuitively, and it is this powerfully intuitive aspect of mind that is embodied by the intellectually-based Air sign of Aquarius.

The Aquarian mind can use these communicative and rational faculties to broadcast the message of oneness and brotherhood to others, through such media as speech and writing. The water from his urn is alive and swarming with ideas that can be beneficially useful for humanity. One modern interpretation is that as Aquarius rules electricity, then its glyph should be interpreted as electrical waves rather than as liquid.

The glyph does not represent a still pool, it depicts waves rippling over water, and it is the winds, or air, which cause the waves to ripple; the Aquarian symbol is therefore suggestive of air currents creating the motion, indicating that Aquarius is indeed a sign of Air and movement, the 'mover' and disseminator of knowledge, the teacher, the inspirational visionary. Being strongly connected with communication, electrical charges and the transmission of information through the activity of brain waves, for example, it seems valid that the Aquarian symbol represents all communication functioning through air currents and electrical impulses - again, symbolised by the two waves.

A further meaning can be derived from the fact that the urn is facing downwards, towards the earth, indicating that knowledge exists on the heavenly plane and must be transmitted to earthlings - and this is the wavelength to which most Aquarians resonate. The Water Bearer's urn and the enlightenment it dispenses, has a strong link with the Aquarian mind, and those Aquarians who are not properly in touch with this concept, or who have presented it to a world which is not quite ready to receive it, can find themselves in a lonely, isolated place. Such feelings of loneliness can lead to feeling out of harmony with 'earthly realms', and a despondent Aquarian will quickly learn how desolate it can be at the top of the proverbial mountain.

THE RUNDOWN ★ SOME QUIRKS, ODDITIES, UNIQUE CHARACTERISTICS AND IDIOSYNCRASIES OF AQUARIUS

"Lots of people like rainbows. Children makes wishes on them, artists paint them, dreamers chase them, but the Aquarian is ahead of everybody. He lives on one …"
Linda Goodman's Sun Signs (1970)

The cerebral nature of Air highlights thought rather than emotion and feeling. Aquarius is largely motivated by reasoning processes. Positive, hot, moist, sanguine and rational, a determined (Fixed) intellectual (Air) approach characterises the sign of Aquarius.

Aquarius is the last of the airy signs, is positive in magnetism, and is ruled by the mighty planets Saturn and Uranus. People born under this sign are generally idealistic, generous and humane, and are quick to relieve the distress or wants of others. Shrewd and intelligent characters, they are acutely sensitive to outside impressions, and are blessed with a natural gift for sensing the magnetic auras of any people or places with which they come into contact. Strong champions of progress in every direction, they long to sweep away that which is corrupt or burdensome and replace it with something more serviceable to the welfare of humanity.

Though blessed with immense reasoning capacity, Aquarius also possesses great intuition and unique prophetic insight, being concerned with the future, rather than what has been before or what is right now. This mind, in spite of its flashy insightfulness, can be surprisingly fixed and difficult to change. Aside from being stubborn, Aquarians are honest and broad-minded, helpful to others, friendly and sociable, and are eager to please. They can also be shy and unpredictable, but are generally thoughtful and outgoing, being very popular with their many friends and acquaintances. While Aquarians have plenty of sensitivity and passion, they believe emotion should be the servant, not the master, of the heart.

The energy of Aquarius holds the 'vision of the future', possessing a mind 'time telescope', and it is an effective agent of social change, stabilised and sophisticated thought processes, and the intellectual capacity to take Capricorn's ideas and break down the structures and boundaries that have been built around them.

The top wave of the Aquarius symbol can be interpreted as standing for the higher mind, with the bottom wave standing for the rational mind. The Aquarian mind's function is to reform structure through vision, applying innovative ideas, and discovery. However, this mind does not dwell in the world of feelings and although well-versed about the human psyche and the human condition on an intellectual level, they rarely wander into the realm of emotions; this keeps the mind 'safe' because it is in its intellectualised position that you can reason with it, whereas feelings cannot be reasoned with, according to the Water Bearer at least.

This sign is one of the most enigmatic signs of the zodiac, and very few people will ever truly understand your motives, your outlook, your nature or your needs (with the exception of other Aquarians perhaps). Although you are cheerful and possess gifts of a high social order, you are also frequently unpredictable, and often surprise others by doing unusual or unexpected things. You have a detached, elusive quality which other people can never seem to pin down, being friendly and remote at the same time. Aquarius represents the vital spiritual power which renews and fertilises all things. However, close, fussy or overly intimate personal relationships may bother you because you are the sign of the global humanitarian, giving you the qualities of the universal lover rather than a personal lover. In fact, you are more effective when functioning within a group, organisation or cause, than when operating within the confines of a personal relationship.

In more ways than one you are a law unto yourself and although you can be very friendly, you do not like to become too deeply involved with other people, even those close to you. You feel most at ease in friendships and relationships where you can keep your distance and independence from others, while still enjoying the pleasure of interactions and exchanges with those you love. For the most part a loner, you treasure your inner freedom far too much to be wiling to surrender your whole self to anyone; a part of you has always to fly above and separate from others, in freer, clearer skies.

Aquarians are simple souls deep down, though most like to trick others into thinking they are complex, mysterious and confident, which is one of the many reasons why you are so misunderstood - which you really don't mind at all, as it allows only those who are perceptive enough to penetrate your veil to come close enough to see the real you.

Aquarians can easily become excitable, for they have a sensitive nervous system. There is an air of contemplative thoughtfulness about you, but this is often coupled with your tendency to talk and chatter and express yourself in every way possible, constantly thinking or speaking about what is going on in your busy mind. You can sometimes lose perspective of your earthly limitations when making plans for the future, and can become impatient and despondent when your actions are hindered or restricted by surrounding circumstances. Being the natural revolutionary and progressive thinker, you are ever eager to overthrow the existing 'system' if it limits the implantation and actualisation of your many theories and visions in any way.

Aquarius is the bohemian of the zodiac, who will try anything at least once and sees nothing wrong with experimentation. The group spirit means a great deal to you, and the feeling of your personal merger with a higher ideal is akin to a religious experience for you. Multifaceted in your social life, you will often do unexpected things which are not sanctioned by the majority. Aquarians may even have a love/hate relationship with one of their associated areas: astrology. The reason for this is because this field, particularly Sun sign astrology, throws them together with other Aquarians, and this threatens their need to be different and individualistic, traits they protect with a deeply ingrained characteristic fixity.

The Aquarian is at its best when working with ideas. Your highest ambition is to make a better world, and this inspiration will keep you going through any obstacle or adversity. Not concerned with image, class or status, independence means more to the Aquarian soul than outward signs of success. You are the sign of the reformer, and this means that you are interested in new ideas, unorthodox trends and original ways of thinking. Independence, freedom in all its forms, individuality and even emotional isolation are necessary for Aquarians to shine their brightest. Sparkling ideas, when combined with emotion, can often become clouded or distorted, and Aquarius doesn't like its outlets or expression of ideas stifled in any way, hence you suppress or store your feelings somewhere else well out of the way. Indeed, Aquarians need to retire from the world at times and to become temporary loners in order to 'recharge' and renew themselves.

You can be temperamental when people or circumstances come into conflict with your many ideas. You can be tenacious when you decide on something, and the fixed quality of Aquarius suggests that you will stubbornly refuse to budge if you are intent on doing something you truly believe to be right. The true Aquarian yearns to be the harbinger of enlightenment, but it is also important that in order to balance your desires and visions with reality, you need to understand that all men are *not* created equal, nor do they all share your conceptions and ideals. Your mission, instead, is to bring new ideas, inventions and social doctrines to the fore so that mankind may experiment with them and come to its own conclusions and solutions; you need only to deliver the 'facts', pouring forth the waters of knowledge from your urn, to start the wheels turning in the right direction.

Refusing to follow the crowd, you dislike interference by others, however helpfully intended, and will accept it only on your own terms; similarly, you may seek advice but will rarely heed it. Possessing strong and attractive personalities, Aquarius is nonetheless the most perplexing sign of the zodiac (a trait shared with Scorpio), and also the most individual and independent; your mind and body must both be as free as the wind.

You are adventurous without being foolhardy, and valiant and self-confident, surrounded by a certain aura of 'knowing', yet blessed with the absence of arrogance. You are unlikely to know defeat, certainly not permanently, and are rarely kept down for long by depression or setbacks.

Your personal style and appearance is usually distinctive and magnetic, attracting those who sense and appreciate your refreshingly quirky uniqueness. Aquarians are indeed unique, but curiously, never in the way everyone else is. Usually popular and well-liked, you are the archetypal good friend and all-rounder, enjoying people both individually and en masse, with a global perspective on humanity and the human condition, but also a gregarious nature towards those in closer circles, endearing you to most and on all levels.

You fall into two principal types: one shy, sensitive, gentle and patient; the other exuberant, lively and exhibitionist, sometimes hiding the substantial depths of your character under a veil of frivolity. Both types are strong-willed, forceful and have strong convictions, and although you seek truth above all things, you are usually honest enough to examine your opinions should you be mistaken in them. You have a breadth of vision, can see both sides of an argument and are unprejudiced and tolerant of others' points of view, even if you do not accept them yourself. In this way you are extremely objective, a quality endowed upon you by the Air element.

Humane, frank, serious minded, intelligent, concise, logical, clear, genial, refined, quick, active, persevering, sometimes ethereal, and ever idealistic, you express yourself with reason, moderation and often a dry brand of humour. Your nature can be difficult at times to pin down, for you are neither cynical nor naïve, neither enthusiastic nor complacent, neither assertive nor timid; and in more ways than one, contradictory.

The freedom-loving Water Bearer can be acutely funny, perverse, original, independent and conceited, but they can also be diplomatic, gentle, sympathetic and reserved. A certain cloud of isolation hangs over the Aquarian, and they are often misunderstood by others, and indeed mankind. That's because mankind hasn't yet caught up with the Aquarian way of thinking, and since your sign lives in the future, you can seem just plain odd and even a bit wacky to more earth-bound, mundane souls. Your Aquarian mind senses this, and it just serves to deepen your sense of isolation, making you apt to wander among the lonely clouds, while the mere mortals around you wonder what you're doing out there - which is usually something along the lines of climbing rainbows, riding a shooting star, wishing upon a distant Sun, reminiscing about the future, re-shaping the past, dreaming up a utopia, swimming in optical illusory mirages, or visualising a society where there are not only round holes but an abundance of square ones too so that everyone may fit in.

However far ahead and out of reach you appear to be, it is always worthwhile for others to try to listen to what the Aquarian is effectively prophesising, for your flashes of insight into tomorrow and beyond have the potential to illuminate the world. Whether you are being social or want to be left strictly alone for periods of solitude and restoration, you'll retain your sharp perception, which is at once both deeper and quicker than everyone else's.

A curious mixture of coolness, charm, aloofness, practicality and eccentric instability, you seem to have an instinctive empathy and affinity with those on differing mind planes, such as the mentally unwell. It is because of your thinly veiled, highly acute nervous system that you have access to such levels of understanding.

You accept neither authority nor convention unless you can be satisfied that there are sound and convincing reasons for them. You see through pretentiousness and pomp and will energetically support causes, sometimes extreme, which oppose tradition, establishment and structure. You are too tolerant and intelligent to become an anarchic revolutionary crusader however, as ultimately you are an original and progressive thinker who seeks innovation and reform above all else, and like to go about it in an unassuming way. Not that you're modest, you are simply unmoved by glory, attention and limelight. Authority also leaves you unmoved and when faced with it, you will regard it with either indifference, deliberate rebellion or even a degree of friendliness or interest, but no amount of courtesy can prevent you from turning the spotlight of truth onto 'reality', for you possess profound integrity and a deep sense of right and wrong, justice and injustice.

You have a powerful desire for a lifestyle that is in some way unique, and are often so devoted to it, and so intent achieving and maintaining independence, that it can be difficult for you to commit to permanent relationships. Really 'knowing' an Aquarian is a matter for debate, for while people of this sign make very good, kind, helpful friends, it soon becomes clear that because they are so private no one really knows much about them. When questioned or cornered, you will usually evade the inquisitor's question or suspicion so successfully, effortlessly and charmingly that it slips by unnoticed such is the elusive charm of Aquarius.

Although you appear absent-minded at times, your thinking is always razor sharp and crystal clear. You also possess an unequalled intuition which gives you a high degree of psychic precognition, and you seem to pick up on your own or others' desires without words, uncovering a need or quality buried so deep that you're even unaware of it yourself. This quality may be somewhat suppressed, however, so that you may get on with the more important business of helping humanity rather than meddling in the affairs of individuals, which holds no appeal to you. In Aquarius, where universal rather than personal objectives are emphasised, the luminous, fiery temperament of the Sun is in its detriment, for the personal will and ego finds little fulfilment in a sign where all are deemed equal.

As well as a strong standing for equality, Aquarians have a great sense of fairness, courage in their ideas and convictions, and passion in their ideals, but by nature they are not very good at reading what's required on a more personal level and may acquire a reputation for being cold and insensitive; they are also prone to teeter on the edge of fanaticism. The Aquarian needs to learn, however, that it can create a prison for itself through its lack of emotional commitment, and deal with the apparent contradiction that freedom actually gains its wings through conscious commitment. To truly soar through the heavens, the Aquarian needs to reconcile this apparent paradox.

The fixed inflexibility of Aquarius is dedicated but uncompromising, for as much as you love change in society and the wider world, you stubbornly refuse to change your own ideas for anybody. Being an essential truth-seeker, you'll seldom tell an outward lie, but you can fool others in very subtle ways; in other words, you will be truthful to a fault, but Aquarian logic dictates that telling a lie is one thing, refraining from telling the whole story is quite another.

Aquarians get credit for being idealists, but you are too clever to be fooled by illusions, swayed by popular opinion, and you can certainly never be accused of blind faith and optimism. You will rarely fight a lost cause for too long, as, being the rational 'realist' that you are ensures your feet are always planted firmly in the ground. You do, however, believe sincerely that a little twisting and tweaking will improve anything, although you can easily be disappointed emotionally because your own high personal ideals cause you to demand more of others than is reasonable; and if disillusioned you may find it hard to forgive.

You are the subtle extremist and the paradoxes don't stop there: you can be a humanitarian or anarchist, protestor or peacemaker, society dropout or the society drop-in centre, genius or fanatic, reputable scientist or mad professor, rebel or social crusader, the liberated or the libertine - or all of the above at the same time! No wonder you make others dizzy and confused! The Aquarius is rarely confused however; rather it is those around it who are left spinning by its frenetic mental activity radiating outwards and electrifying those who are courageous enough to come in close enough to really feel it. But if those others do take the time to listen to you, they will actually catch a glimpse of the future, for it is here the true and pure Aquarius dwells.

Aquarians usually possess an above average intelligence, enhanced by their inventive, progressive and futuristic thinking. The Air element expresses itself in Aquarius as aloof detachment and lack of deep personal involvement, which allows the Aquarian to indulge their eccentricities and spread their trademark friendliness even further. Being essentially detached and impersonal, expressions of deep feelings won't come easily to an Aquarian, and the line between love and friendship is all but invisible to the Water Bearer's soul. The Aquarian belongs to everyone, yet to no one; love can be wild and adventurous, but there will always be an elusive quality about it, and you will do everything you can to avoid great displays of intimacy.

From time to time, real brilliance can emerge from Aquarians, and anyone close to such individuals should be careful not to write them off as harmless eccentrics. Though rarely does an Aquarian see themself as an eccentric, just a little ahead of their time and not fully understood. Blessed with such an ingenious mind, you should develop your inborn originality, since you can be very creative. This, coupled with your need to have a distinctively individual lifestyle, unhindered by commitments and authority, are likely to provide your greatest motivations to succeed.

Aquarians can quite easily rise from obscurity to develop high-minded purposes and strong characters. Your self-reliance, gifted intellect, unique way of looking at things, understated confidence and your inner 'knowing' that you are right are assets which could be used to climb skyward. Indeed these are the qualities that can lay the foundation of your success, and once your ambition is sparked, you are capable of scaling unprecedented heights.

You have a tendency to indolence however, and if you delay or treat life lazily, you will never achieve the great heights your mind is capable of achieving. Your unassuming nature and lack of boastfulness and ego are also assets which can be used to climb skyward. Ultimately, Aquarians are dedicated and humane champions to their causes, with strong ideals and convictions, and above all, forever seeking the truth - which always resides in tomorrow.

THE THREE DECANS OF AQUARIUS

Decans are thirty-six groups of stars that rise in a particular order on the horizon throughout each Earth rotation. These decans were developed in Egypt thousands of years ago. The rising of each decan marked the beginning of a new 'decanal hour' of the night for these ancient people, and eventually three decans were assigned to each zodiac sign. Each decan covers ten degrees of the zodiac wheel, and is ruled by different planetary rulers that rule over the other two signs of the same element. Decans continued to be used throughout the Ages, in astrology and in magic, but many modern astrologers, for whatever reasons, tend to disregard them. Below are brief descriptions for each decan of Aquarius. Which one do you belong to? Can you relate to the description and the energies of your decan's ruling planet?

FIRST DECAN AQUARIUS ★ January 21 - 30

RULER ★ Venus (traditional *) / Uranus (modern)

Birthdays in this decan range from 21st to 30th January. This is the Aquarius decan, ruled by Uranus and Venus *. Aquarians born during this decan possess an original, inventive mind which comes up with innovative ideas and engages in progressive thinking. Your concepts, views and beliefs are often seen as unusual, futuristic or avant-garde. You thrive when around many other people and shine your brightest when you are at parties and social gatherings. You love meeting new people, enjoying new experiences, and are attractive and fascinating to others, who you easily entrance and beguile with your uniqueness, wit and charm. You dislike being constrained by conventions and personal relationships, and need regular time by yourself in your own inner world. You may come across as weird or eccentric to others, and always live truthfully and unwaveringly by your own unique code.

First decan Aquarians' three special Tarot cards are ★ The Star, King of Swords & Five of Swords

SECOND DECAN AQUARIUS ★ January 31 - February 9

RULER ★ Mercury (traditional *) / Mercury (modern)

Birthdays in this decan range from 31st January to 9th February. This is the Gemini decan, ruled by Mercury. Aquarians born during this decan have good reasoning ability, a ready wit, and an ability to reach out to people with a mental and intellectual approach. You are likely to be changeable, versatile and enjoy variety and change. This influence also makes you imaginative, honest, open and smart, and an analytical thinker who makes decisions based on your head rather than your heart. Naturally academic and scholarly, you love study, both formal and informal (incidental) and you tend to live your life at a fast pace, preferring quick results to whatever you apply your mind to. Second decan Aquarians are characterised by openness, sociability and imagination, making you a gifted communicator and excellent at pursuits such as creative writing. You can use the power of words to your advantage, getting your message across eloquently and convincingly. Intelligent, clear-thinking and quick-witted, what others see is what they get with you, as you have no hidden agenda; Aquarian frankness and 'truth' is at its purest under the influence of clever Mercury, and you are always one step ahead of others in your thinking.

Second decan Aquarians' three special Tarot cards are ★ The Star, King of Swords & Six of Swords

THIRD DECAN AQUARIUS ★ February 10 - 19

RULER ★ Moon (traditional *) / Venus (modern)

Birthdays in this decan range from 10th February to 19th February. This is the Libra decan, ruled by Venus and the Moon *. Aquarians born during this decan are characterised by impulsivity, charm and romanticism. With a constant need for social stimulation and excitement, you love to explore many fascinating ideas and interests. A natural romantic, love plays a big part in your life, and you are charming and magnetising, attracting many admirers to you, but your need for change and your natural restlessness can prove a challenge to achieving sustained long-term relationships. Bright, breezy and charismatic, you enjoy attention from others and sharing your thoughts, affection and concepts. Being so mysterious and intriguing, many will try and figure you out, but very few will succeed, for your true nature is often hidden. You are the most sensitive and emotional of the Aquarian decans, and although easily bored, you are unerringly generous to those you love, and will always give your time, love and energy to them unconditionally.

Third decan Aquarians' three special Tarot cards are
★ The Star, Knight of Cups & Seven of Swords

* The decan's traditional ruler based on the Chaldean order of the planets

YOUR ELEMENT ★ AIR

★ The Intellectual Group ★

The path to BROTHERHOOD

Focused on Mental & Social Interactions

Key Attributes ★ Communication, intelligence, reason, perspective, renewal, thought, logic

Symbolism ★ Clear thought, communication, study, connection to the Universals

Governed by ★ The Mind and the Psyche

Air Characteristics ★ Intelligent, wise, thoughtful, analytical, detached, objective

★ KEYWORDS ★

Broad-minded, fair, objective, refined, ideas-oriented, communicative, observant, versatile, rational, theoretical, social, learning-oriented, impersonal, logical, connecting, detached, active-minded, clever, curious, impartial, cooperative, abstract, integrating, networking, analytical, relationship-oriented

Air is the mental principle. It seeks to share and communicate ideas to others. Air is associated with the thinking function and its motivating force is intellectual stimulation. It is characterised by intellect, communication and aspiration. Air signs are rational and logical, seeking mental understanding and experiencing life through the mind. They are also objective and 'head-orientated', sometimes to the detriment of their emotions and intuition.

The three Air signs are Gemini the Twins, Libra the Scales and Aquarius the Water Bearer. In the horoscope wheel, Gemini represents personal development, Libra represents interpersonal development, and Aquarius represents transpersonal development. The Air signs are masculine in polarity, extroverted in expression and are aligned with the realms of relationships and connections of all kinds.

The Air element is connected to understanding, intellectual concepts, innovations, insight, mental rapport, technology, synthesising information, ideas, communication, and knowledge. As air has no boundaries, it can be difficult for this element to accept boundaries established by others. It is objective, gives a sense of separation through interdependence, is sophisticated and is linked to the past, present *and* future. It seeks mental rapport and stimulation above all else, and has a conscious sense of knowing.

This element is detached, impersonal, separate, represents breath and life, is an ideas perfectionist, is judging, assessing, collating, paradoxical, space-seeking, freedom-seeking, flighty, has an approach/avoidance element, develops ways to communicate, is an observer/spectator, gossiper, is an excellent witness to the human experience, equality-idealist, dual-natured, has difficulty with intimacy, is dissociative in the face of challenge, aware, conscious, has an urge to relate and 'share', is socially inclined, witty, has perspective, keeps its distance, is changeable, fair, inspiring, learning, opinionated and has an attitude of "knowledge is power."

Airy temperaments excel at clear, objective reasoning and have a capacity for lively, intelligent communication and the exchange of ideas. These types are gregarious, civilised, curious, cooperative, casual, fun-loving and sociable.

However, you can be overly intellectual, objective and rational, uncomfortable with feelings, and too often trust your head before your heart. Other weaknesses that may trip you up occasionally are that you have a tendency to be scattered, unfocused, restless, unrealistic, detached, distant, impersonal, nervous, unstable, inconsistent, spacey, erratic, whimsical, fickle, impractical, superficial, opinionated, dogmatic, impulsive, skittish, 'mercurial', disembodied, a chatterbox, have an overactive mind and can't be tied down.

As the element suggests, airy spirits are constantly on the move, shifting, changing and evolving. Air signs are generally unnerved by states of flux, as movement is a chance for growth and exploration to these inquisitive souls. Independent, open-minded and spontaneous, air signs loathe restrictions and anything which curtails their freedom, especially of thought. They love to broaden their horizons through circulating amongst people, places and experiences, as understanding others and their surroundings is paramount to making sense of their existence.

Air signs rely heavily on reason, logic and objectivity. This enables the cerebral Air signs to make fair and objective assessments, but this intellectualisation of thought and feeling can also make them come across as detached and unemotional. As they have a strong need for novel and perpetual stimulation, Air signs tend to be restless and can suffer from nerve-related upsets. Blessed with outgoing and naturally expressive personalities, they are highly sociable as well as good communicators. Air signs enjoy the company of others and love engaging in hearty, interesting conversations through which they can gain knowledge and exchange ideas. Impartial by nature, they often make great mediators in relationships or families and having an upbeat, generally uncomplicated nature means Air signs also have a natural talent for diffusing tense situations and lifting the spirits of others.

HOW YOU CAN GET IN TOUCH WITH YOUR AIR ENERGY

"When we are present with and summon the magic of Air, we gain wings"

★ Spend time in open, fresh, clean air regularly

★ Spend time in wide open spaces and engage in outdoor activities that make use of the air around you, such as flying a kite or ballooning

★ Learn Prana-, Chi- or Ki-related disciplines, martial arts, meditation and yoga that focus on breathing, focus, detachment and concentration

★ Read as much as you can, be an eternal student

★ Develop your networking skills

★ Throw intellectual dinner parties

★ Join a discussion group or an online Internet chatroom

★ Practice deep breathing

★ Learn about meteorology, cloud formations, the atmosphere and weather

★ Use a negative ion machine, humidifier or air purifier in your home

★ Don't smoke, or if you do, quit

★ Sleep on an air mattress

★ Meditate on the Swords suit in the Tarot (the Swords suit represents the Air element)

★ Take a course - in anything and everything!

★ Know a little bit about everything

★ Write

★ Visit the library on a regular basis; join a book discussion group

★ Look after your lungs, other components of your respiratory system, and your nervous system

★ Take a course, learn a language, or otherwise make a commitment to a learning activity which requires discipline, focus and mental energy

★ Take a course on improving your relationships

★ Hire a jumping castle and invite your friends over

★ Jump on a trampoline

★ Practice public speaking often, even in front of a mirror

★ Forget your mind chatter and allow your heart to lead occasionally; it always knows where to go

YOUR MODE ★ FIXED

This mode signifies the manifestation of purpose. It is associated with stabilisation, depth, preservation, persistence, loyalty and strength of will. You operate with dedication and determination. Fixed signs are a forceful group, able to follow their will and demonstrate fixity. You are enduring, but may be rigid and single-minded. You work hard to consolidate and preserve the things that matter to you, but you can also be inflexible and resistant to change. Your energy and nature is concrete, limited, stable, set in its ways, purposeful, conscientious, consistent, determined, enduring, stubborn, has a sense of routine, ritual, control, innate caution, rigidity, unimpulsive, opinionated, unchanging, and you are generally strong in opinions, habits, likes and dislikes. Not easily distracted, you always keep your eyes on the prize, but you have a tendency to brood or to become stuck in a rut. The fixed mode indicates the midpoints of the seasons, which are very strong ritualistic times and 'fixed points', signifying points of power in the zodiac.

YOUR RULING PLANET ★ URANUS

The Great Awakener & Divine Rebel

Transcendental ★ Associated with Change, Disruption and Shock ★ 84 Year Cycle

★ KEY WORDS ★

Intuition, electrifying force, innovation, disruption, higher or psychic functions, individuality, cosmic consciousness, inventions, shock, sudden or unexpected change, originality, electricity, revolution!

★ KEY CONCEPTS ★

★ The intuitive faculties, the Sixth Sense ★

★ The bohemian, the beatnik, the hippie, the nonconformist ★

★ The inventor, the 'mad scientist', the revolutionary, the anarchist ★

★ Destroyer of old ideologies, ways of life, concepts and structures ★

★ The global crusader, the social reformer ★

★ The embracer of Brotherhood, the humanitarian ★

★ The force for the awakening of the higher consciousness: individually, collectively and universally ★

★ He who marches to the beat of his own drum ★

Uranus was discovered during the American and French revolutions in 1781, correlating it with the social themes of the time: freedom, independence, revolution and rebellion. It is therefore fitting that Uranus, which sits beyond Saturn, should represent a break from tradition and barriers, and a certain emancipation from the structures and order that Saturn imposes. Discovered by musician and astronomer William Herschel, Uranus was at first believed to be a comet until further investigation confirmed its planetary nature. Its discovery was a startling revelation for the fields of astronomy and astrology, as the two disciplines believed the solar system extended only to the limit of Saturn's orbit.

Uranus offers a welcome change from its neighbouring planet Saturn, giving us a chance to seize our freedom, break free, be progressive and enhance our creativity. People born under the sign of Aquarius are particularly sensitive to its influence, and being born with an (often) emphasised Uranus factor makes them susceptible to being extremely stimulated most of the time, living in a constant state of wired or other-worldly energy.

Uranus is an erratic planet, orbiting on its axis at a 90 degree angle, different from the way everything else in the solar system behaves, giving a good allusion to the nature of the Uranian mind: a different way of 'spinning' to almost everything and everyone around it. The Aquarian mind seems to have adopted this quirk from its ruling planet.

Uranus is the first of the 'impersonal' planets and rules less intimate relationships such as friendships and acquaintanceships. It also denotes memberships of clubs, societies, groups and political organisations, and is associated with modern inventions such as electricity, computers, aviation, television, and the discovery of radiation. Concerned with the realm of ideas and the intellect, it exudes an air of coolness and logic. But most of all, this planet's role is to break down the established 'order' and replace it with experimental, novel or idealistic regimes - whether these are applied to the wider world, or in our personal lives. It acts to break up the crystallisation that Saturn has imposed, and stands for originality, shock, inspiration, dynamic self-expression, will and the ability to synthesise. It also acts to electrify, galvanise, vivify, awaken and mobilise, often working in a spasmodic, unexpected fashion, but highly effective as an agent of change nonetheless. It signifies unusual characters, inventors, electricians, and those with transcendental interests. Uranus is a political planet which seeks to change and manoeuvre the world into new ways of thinking and *being*.

Before the discovery of the three outer planets which lay beyond the detection of the naked eye, the ruler of Aquarius was Saturn. Today, after the discovery of Uranus, Saturn is regarded as Aquarius's secondary or traditional ruler. Indeed, very old astrology texts describe Aquarians in Saturnian terms, which seems odd to most now, given the Aquarian temperament is regarded as the polar opposite of everything traditional or Saturnian. Occasionally, however, you may still meet with an Aquarian who is cautious, conservative, even dull, slow-going, melancholy, quiet, thoughtful, deep, reticent and restrained in their passions; you may even be one of these types yourself! But more often than not, a typical Aquarian will have been endowed with all that is Uranian: unpredictable, convention-defying, unusual, occasionally shocking, different, eccentric and in extreme cases, that one oddball in the crowd we all know and love. It is Uranus's influence which helps make the Water Bearer the prophet, social reformer, brilliant thinker and free spirit that he or she doubtless is.

Uranus, the primal Greek God who ruled the sky and the personification of the Greek heaven, is brilliant and loves the original and the unconventional, whether it be astonishing invention or acts of wilful rebellion. In short, Uranus 'shakes it up'. Uranus is the 'rebel' and the 'outsider' and corresponds with our urge to break down constraints of the past; in the individual context, this can mean breaking old patterns of behaviour. On a collective level, but stemming from the individual, it signifies the urge for reform, revolution, change and the realisation of new ideas.

It rules the abnormal, aircraft, astrology, brotherhood, electrical engineers, transformers, agitators, airports, divorce, alarms, homosexuality, anarchy, freaks, altruism, freedom, appliances, microphones, disorder, astronomy, stereograms, avant garde, aviation, the unexpected, batteries, bohemia, experiments, boycotts, changes, circulation, tornadoes, computers, shocks, spark plugs, contradictions, convulsions, cranks, informalities, peculiarities, aliens, prodigies, interruptions, discoveries, innovations, disruptions, turbines, twitching, unconventionality, dynamo, earthquakes, spasms, eccentricities, electricity, electronics, ankles, elopement, advanced ideas, erratic behaviours, exile, sonar, 'the uninvited', upheavals, upsets, extraordinary, flashes, sudden, foreign, fugitives, gales, elevators, hippies, impulses, independence, inventions, liberation, libertine, lightning, metaphysics, humanism, the new and modern, radar, strikes, radiators, nonconformists, strangeness, novelties, occultism, originality, outlaws, paradoxes, radicalism, radios, rebels, reform, generators, genius, helicopters, research, runaways, scientists, separations, surprises, switchboards, television, trespassing, hurricanes, and X-rays. I'm sure you get the idea!

Uranus, as one of the three outer or generational planets, is regarded as a 'planet of a higher octave', along with Neptune and Pluto. These higher octave forces account for those flashes of inspiration we are occasionally jolted with, when we become especially aware of our life's purpose, albeit usually only very fleetingly - unless of course you are an Aquarian!

Uranus embodies esoteric principles which symbolise vibrations of cosmic energy that affect whole generations and collective mankind, rather than touching us on a personal level; however Aquarians and other people whose Uranus is strongly placed or emphasised in their birth chart, can certainly be individually affected by this planet's influence.

Uranus is Mercury's higher octave, and although both function on an intellectual level, Mercury rules the everyday and logic, while Uranus rules intuition and sees far further than the immediate moment and environment. It could also be said that Mercury is the trickster, Uranus the magician. Here, the versatile is raised to the volatile. Uranus is not content with leading the way along existing roads; instead, it will carve a new channel through the mountains where nobody thought roads could ever be created. Sometimes this road takes unexpected twists and turns; such is the nature of this unpredictable planet.

But Uranus doesn't *make* us believe in magic, for that belief already exists within most of us, instead it reinforces our belief in it, by dropping moments of serendipity, dazzling insights or unexpected surprises into our laps. Uranus may pull rabbits out of the cosmic hat and enchant us with its inexplicable genius, but it is also capable of pulling the magical carpet out from under us just as suddenly, leaving us shocked and a little bewildered. Life - and Uranus - has a way of doing that.

Aquarians are said to be ahead of their time, and therefore slightly out of sync with the surrounding world. The Industrial Revolution, a historical period which followed the discovery of Uranus, ushered in the apparent Age of Enlightenment, or at least the Age of Technology. Ever since that period of time, it has been suggested that we are entering the cusp of the Age of Aquarius, and while we are not all the way into it yet, we are certainly in transition. Considering that an astrological age takes around 2,100 years to complete, the cusp can take a couple of hundred years. The reason the Age of Aquarius has been so glorified and embraced with mounting excitement, is that Uranus rules this sign. We can expect a Uranian rush of energy, thrills, adventure, progress, changes and above all, advancement. This planet has a tendency of sending us rushing off in all directions to find the gold at the end of the rainbow, which is yet to be found - but the pot of gold that the Age of Aquarius stands for is nearly upon us. In fact Aquarians are already in firm possession of it, as they are living already in that rosy-coloured utopian future its profound influence promises us all.

In today's world, many Aquarian-themed ideas have emerged, and Aquarian technologies have brought about so much information that we can safely label our times the 'Age of Information'. Although we are not yet living in the Age of Aquarius, the concepts of the Water Bearer have been emerging more strongly as each new decade unfolds, and humanity is slowly making the great shift towards seeing each individual as a part of the whole. Uranus has a grand plan, an aspiration to roll out a new spiral of evolutionary accomplishment for humanity, and will indeed live it out through those upon whom it bestows the gift of effecting this whole-world change to - namely, Aquarians.

Uranus is the planet which embodies the sixth sense, and Aquarians are often gifted with the flashes of insight that are characteristic of the higher, spiritual faculties of the mind. Uranian individuals are therefore blessed with the futuristic and brilliant intellect that a strong Uranian influence implies, especially if at the time of your birth Uranus was well-placed in the sky in relation to Mercury, the two combining forces to indicate genius.

Revolutionary by nature, true Uranians are idealistic and work towards the betterment of humanity, never satisfied with past traditions or present 'realities'. Uranus can manifest in us individually as erratic rebellion or the inner peace of simply 'being' an individual. It indicates the launching of oneself or one's ideas into a new environment, taking the risk for change, and disconnection in order to be able to stand back and see more clearly. It signifies one's level of individuality, freedom, extremism, radicalism, reformist side, anarchism, fanaticism, electricity, inventiveness and unpredictability. It is concerned with the collective mind, illumination, awakening, unconventionality and new discoveries. It is the humanitarian urge, the great 'awakener' in social change and on a personal, individual level it can awaken our 'dormant' side, understanding things conceptually and with vision. Essentially uncomfortable with feelings, it has a detached understanding of the world. Uranus is what gives us sudden flashes of inspiration, ideas and thoughts, and signifies our instinctive understanding of what may be hidden and unseen, and of what is not known by the conscious mind.

Uranus, being the ruler of Aquarius, the sign which has long been associated with pouring forth from heaven the 'waters of life' onto humanity, lends a prophetic and futuristic slant to the Water Bearer's mind. However, the sheer force of Uranian creativity seldom reaches its pure 'cosmic' form, as pure creative power can cause turbulence and disturbance in the earthly human psyche, and this turbulence usually manifests as acts of rebellion against the past, the 'establishment' and traditional structures rather than explosive revelation.

The Uranus influence upon the Aquarian soul urges the Water Bearer to enlighten others and certainly to pour the waters of knowledge onto his fellow humans, friend or foe. Not that Aquarians have many, or indeed any, enemies, for ignorance to these souls is not bliss but potential devastation. Being ever tolerant, they are rarely prejudiced and do not discriminate; there is more than enough water in their urn to soften and water the arid fields of ignorance and societal discord.

The Uranian character has a pioneering spirit and super consciousness has often arrived after the sacrifice of personal or earthly life for these individuals, and pure Uranian types have contributed significantly to the progressive and evolutionary process of life across the globe. Indeed, Uranus is the iconoclast and the divine rebel of the solar system, and he drives the human will through his creative powers. In fact, according to mythology, he started out as a creator before he became the rebel of the skies.

The position of Uranus in your birth chart will tell you about your levels of social rebelliousness, but being an Aquarian, it's a pretty sure bet that this planet exerts a somewhat significant influence upon you regardless. Bohemianism (also a product of the spiritual Neptune), a yearning for freedom, and new age progressive thinking all form part of the typical Aquarian style; although you may not be socially rebellious, your urge for freedom may be expressed on an internal level rather than through lifestyle. As an inherent rebel, however, Uranus will ensure that your spirit will live according to its own rules, in whatever form of expression it manifests.

Being prominent in your psyche as Aquarius's modern ruling planet, Uranus gives you a heightened intellect, access to brilliant ideas and a sense of the unusual and 'different'. An original thinker with often lightning flash thoughts, you love the unpredictable side of life, sometimes revelling in chaos, upheavals or change, which is when you come into your own. You instinctively know how to handle crises and are able to keep a cool head about you when all around are losing theirs.

Uranus, along with Jupiter, is associated with lightning, and bestows the Aquarian with those lightning bolt thinking processes. However, these thoughts may never make it to earth, and the sense of frustration that the soaring Aquarian spirit so often experiences, is due to its flying high among the nebulae, keenly aware of the universal order of the cosmos, but trapped in an earthly body that is typically restricted and tied up in chains. Those Uranian characters who are unable to find a way to reconcile this creative dilemma can often suffer isolation and loneliness, for when one has flown though or resided in the kingdoms of greatness, the real world beneath one's feet can be a very lonely place.

Uranian energy, magnetism and attraction is often at work in matters of love. Romantic adventures that begin under a strong Uranian influence often end as intensely and abruptly as they began. Aquarians need to guard against this erratic and unpredictable influence, which has a particularly strong effect upon their lives and characters. This is especially true during natal transitions to your ruling planet, when you may find yourself overwhelmingly drawn to someone's magnetic field or 'aura', only to be brought back down to earth and reality once the transit is complete. These transit periods are often characterised by a feeling of being elevated to euphoric states and heavenly heights, but Uranus has a way of delivering the unexpected with its characteristic shock value.

A strong Uranus makes for a friendly, independent, kind, but rather detached and sometimes isolated character who possesses an inventive brain and a broad, far-seeing mind. However, you may also be obstinate and have a determination to live your life in your own way. Your unorthodox approach to situations and your embedded rebellious tendencies, however well hidden or misunderstood by others, are usually used for the betterment of others' lives and the advancement of society in general, e.g. through invention and innovative ideas. You have a pure heart which is firmly in the right place, and are well-intentioned, especially when it comes to defending the 'underdog'. Above all, you seek and *live* the truth, despite your employing of unusual methods to capture its essence.

All significant Uranus aspects can have a profound effect upon our lives. It takes 84 years to fully return to the position it was in at the time of our birth. Therefore, approximately every 20 to 21 years, it will form a significant aspect to its natal position, with the first square aspect occurring at 21 years of age, when the spirit of rebellion and 'breaking free' is at its height. At around the age of 42, it forms an opposition to its natal position, and this is when we start to really assess and search ourselves to work out whether or not we have achieved our goals or realised our dreams. Wisdom may very well teach us that this is the time to shift the focus of our attention from purely material or worldly concerns, to more spiritual, creative and individuated goals, which is much more aligned with Uranus's nature. The final square occurs at the age of approximately 63, and significantly, this is around the age of retirement, a time to break free from the restrictions of working life and paying off a traditional mortgage or other material goals. Uranus returns to its own natal position when we are 84, usually the end of the life span - that's if we don't miss it altogether through death or dementia. These are the years when arguably truly magical things can happen for us. If we were to take a cue from native tribes who honour, respect and revere their elders, we may even experience the ultimate Uranian enlightenment of this phase of life, which we were destined to meet. Symbolically, this final Uranian infusion suggests a potential for spiritual re-birth, particularly for the Aquarian spirit, and a new adventure in detaching ourselves at last from the world altogether in order to fix our sights upon greener and freer horizons.

This Uranian energy and influence, throughout your whole life, gives Aquarians the 'gifts' of vision, originality, futuristic thinking, and eccentricity, giving the potential to be the impactful 'outsider', and the bringer of hope and messages society most needs to hear. Too much of this Uranian energy can make one anarchistic, fanatical, contrary, unpredictable, inflexible and overly eccentric, to the point of 'dropping out' of or being rejected by society. But the Aquarian always knows what's best for his or her own soul; after all, your motto is "I Know," because deep down, you really do *know*, even if you can never quite manage to articulate *what* it is exactly that you know. How will *you* use your phenomenally powerful Uranian influence?

YOUR HOUSE IN THE HOROSCOPE ★ THE ELEVENTH HOUSE

The horoscope, or birth chart, is divided into twelve sections called houses. Each house governs a different area or 'department' of life, such as relationships, career, leisure and even karma. The reason for this division of the Earth into houses can be understood when we consider that the Sun's rays affect us differently in the morning, at noon and at night, and also in summer and winter, and if we study the cause, we will readily observe that it is the angle at which the ray strikes us or the Earth which produces that difference in effect. Similarly with the stellar rays astrologers have observed that a child born at or near midday, when the Sun's rays strike the birthplace from the Tenth House, has an improved chance of public or career advancement in life than one born after sunset. By similar observations and tabulations it has been found that the other planetary rays affect the various departments of life when their ray is projected through the other houses, and therefore each house is said to 'rule' or govern certain departments of the human life experience.

The Eleventh House, ruled by Aquarius, is the house of friendships, acquaintanceships, groups, social life, group involvement, social affinities, clubs and organisations, collectives, networking, social conscience, social causes, progress, ideals, global awareness, progress, political visions, and our hopes, wishes and aspirations.

As an Air sign, this is one of the three Houses of Relationships. But where Gemini is concerned with relationships on a personal level and Libra on an interpersonal level, the Aquarius-ruled Eleventh House is concerned with relationships on a transpersonal, or wider-reaching, level.

This house tells us much about our social life and work associates. On a personal level, the eleventh sphere of the wheel also reveals how we pursue our ideals, hopes, dreams and aspirations, and gives us hints about how we can incorporate other people socially and within groups, to help us reach our highest goals and ideals, on both a personal and (more often) collective level. It also shows what we may achieve by tailoring our personal goals to the needs of society, and teaches us that the endeavours of a coordinated group can achieve more than the sum of several individual efforts. Planets in this house indicate the type of friends who attract us and where we find common interests with others.

This house is not concerned with self-gratification or personal pleasure like its opposite Leo's Fifth House is; instead it operates in an impersonal sphere of life, dealing with cerebral spirituality and global-realisation rather than self-actualisation.

In the Eleventh House we see how we integrate into the group; how we operate within the larger system. The traditional name for this house was in fact the House of Hopes, Dreams and Wishes. It can also be described as the realm of communal spirit, the House of Brotherhood, or the House of Friends and Idealism.

If the Eleventh House influence is strong in the birth chart, such as being born under an Aquarian Sun, we will be inclined to choose forms of self-expression which involve the group more so than the individual. The Eleventh House ensures that we pour out our precious waters of consciousness where they are needed the most: upon groups and societies, and the world at large. The global community, after all, is a perpetually thirsty place, ever in need of a refreshing drink.

YOUR OPPOSITE SIGN ★ LEO

WHAT YOU CAN LEARN FROM THE LION

Although the word 'opposite' conjures up feelings of separateness and differences, the astrological polarities should not be seen as two signs in conflict with each other - their positive expression is to create a natural balance and equilibrium. Each sign has something to learn from its opposite, but also has a contribution to make towards the other sign's more evolved expression. The Fifth (Leo) and the Eleventh (Aquarius) House polarity is concerned with personal creativity versus group creativity and contribution.

Positive and fixed, the balance of this polarity is between the artist and the scientist, the individual and the group, the strong ego and the underdeveloped ego, the autocrat and the democrat. Leo is self-centred and radiates self-confidence like the Sun radiates warmth, while the pure Aquarian is only one cog in a vast operating system and is not motivated by self-interest or lofty, self-serving ambitions. Leo can be an egotistical and arrogant dictator who may become oblivious to the existence of those 'beneath' him, unless of course they serve as exploitable followers. On the other hand, Aquarius looks after the rights of others he considers his 'brothers', ever upholding causes and personal ideals that work towards the benefit of all. But the Aquarian can easily lose his personal identity by over-emphasising the needs of the group and must therefore look towards the creative individuality of Leo for support.

The modern associations between Aquarius and Uranus has given this sign an often exaggerated reputation for being rebellious, difficult, eccentric, perverse and unstable. All of these negative traits and behaviours arise as extreme manifestations in individuals who have not yet found their centre - or their heart. This is Leo's domain, and from this very centre it can teach a lot to its Water Bearer friends.

The two houses ruled by Leo and Aquarius in the horoscope are the Fifth and Eleventh houses. The Fifth House is where a person consolidates and expresses his individuality and outer identity through various leisurely and creative pleasures, whereas the eleventh house is a less personal, more widely varying expression of one's individuality - usually concerning the individual in the context of a group or wider society. It indicates one's altruistic attitudes and activities, friendships, social connections and broad motivations and aspirations, while the opposing Fifth

House is much more individually-centred and self-oriented.

Although the Sun is in detriment in the sign of Aquarius (being opposite Leo, which is ruled by the Sun), the Water Bearer will usually still manage to make their mark on the world, albeit in a less 'showy' way than their Lion opposite. Nonetheless, being in detriment, the Sun is quite weak in the sign of the Water Bearer, and Aquarians may feel at times (or all of the time) lacking in self-confidence and unsure of themselves, and shun the limelight. You may also suffer a weak or ineffective ego, and find it difficult to assert yourself and truly 'shine' or stand tall and proud. These are Leo's forte; the Lion can certainly teach you lessons in straightening your back, lifting your chin up and looking upwards to the Sun.

Aquarius is primarily an impersonal and group-oriented sign, and operates according to thinking principles. It is concerned with the energies of the group rather than with the personal creative unfolding of the individual. Leo is individualistic and uninterested in the group; it seeks above all to become what it envisions as its own heroic potential. Aquarius is logical, consistent and principled; Leo is dramatic, spontaneous, intuitive and seeks myth rather than fact. Aquarius believes the 'whole' is more important than the parts which compose it, seeking hard facts, logical principles and behaves with the benefit of the collective or the 'group' in mind; Leo seeks joy, self-expression, spontaneity, the right to believe in magic and to bring fairy tales alive on life's vast stage. Aquarius, on the other hand, with its innately broader viewpoint, will promptly wipe out the individual if it runs too rampant in life's theatre.

The creative individual, intent on developing his own uniqueness and creative power (Leo), seeks to become aware of the larger human family of which he is a part, so that he may offer his creative gifts with an objective understanding of their value to others (Aquarius). Aquarius, being a group-conscious individual, is aware of the importance of the needs of others around him, but needs to develop a stronger ego, true self-confidence, a greater sense of his own value and creativity so that he has something of his own to offer, which is the energy he can learn from Leo.

To evolve to your fullest potential, you need to learn the Lion's lessons of expressing your life force creatively from deep within your heart and thus empower your soul. Your karmic goal is to become heart-centred and empowered. In order to develop your true highest potential and follow your soul's true path, your soul needs to learn how to give and receive affection more freely, allow your natural warmth to shine through and trust in your heart rather than your head. Aquarians tend to rely mostly on their intellectual reasoning to make decisions when they've reached a crossroads, and are often in need of some hearty lessons from the Lion.

Being an Aquarian, you may also behave in a way that is self-preserving or protective of yourself, as you are afraid your ideas may not be accepted, but if you work on emanating warmth to others and swallowing your intellectual pride, you will be more open to receiving love and abundance in all its forms. You also need to work on being more assertive and expressive and a little bit more 'bossy' than you may feel comfortable with. Taking the lead and being in the limelight may feel awkward for you as it is not something the Aquarian soul is well acquainted with, but once you are a bit more practised in these areas, your life's journey will reflect back to you greater success and stronger meaning.

Your creative talents need to be tapped into to allow the real *you* to flow more naturally through life. Having suppressed these creative outlets in the past, perhaps thinking that they are not rational, you have put your mind before your true instincts, which are telling you to flower into a more creative and outwardly expressive person.

Typical of Aquarius, periods of low self esteem and a weak ego have likely been a huge hindrance for you so far on your life's path, so it would be really helpful for you to learn some self-confidence which will transform your life with amazing results. Being outwardly expressive and demonstrative may be difficult for you in the beginning, but your soul's inner voice is telling you that these need working on. Leo is sitting across the astrological table from you, and this generous, giving spirit will happily provide the light you need for the heart-centred path ahead.

Leo can teach you the value of relating to children, romance, play time, affection, leisure, relaxing, a willingness to take risks, and indulging in personal pleasures. They can also encourage in you a greater desire to express yourself creatively, to channel your creative energies more effectively, and to play with and nurture your inner child more often.

Ultimately, you need to come out of your shell and announce your arrival to the world, in true Leo style! And you can be guaranteed that as you come out from behind those curtains, somewhere in the audience, one very proud Lion, symbolically or real, will be the first to applaud your grand entrance. The whole pride might even attend your opening night if you're super lucky.

WHAT THE LION CAN ULTIMATELY TEACH THE WATER BEARER

Warmth, self-confidence, how to demonstrate affection more openly, individual focus, ego-examination, how to enjoy genuine leisure and pleasure, how to develop a stronger ego, creativity, and to live with more emphasis on the heart than the head.

MAGIC, DRAWING, ATTRACTION, SPELLS, RITUALS, WISHING & POWER

What is Magic?

Magic is a kind of special energy that is beyond description, and like most kinds of energy it has its own rules and ways of being manipulated. It remains an elusive term, and no definition has ever really found universal acceptance. Attempts to separate it from superstition, religion and other-worldly phenomena on the one hand, and 'science' on the other, are ridden with difficulties. However slippery the term 'magic' might be, there is a general agreement that most of us wish for more of it in our lives and often fall short of achieving this wish.

Those performing spells, 'asking the Universe', wishing, praying or undertaking rituals, are using this very special energy to draw things to them. Learning to manipulate energy in these ways is never hard (and shouldn't be), but it can be complex and does require knowledge, practice, creativity, patience and above all, imagination. Most of us use simple magic every day, whether by saying little prayers, making wishes, visualising, and exchanging - sending out and receiving - good, positive or hopeful vibes. When you understand that all the forces and magic you need are *within* you, and you learn to believe in that power, you are then able to make all manner of changes to your life and your self.

Magic is an invisible force which connects and permeates everything. Every thought you have and every action you take, will affect the strength of this force, and can be influenced and directed towards a specific purpose by using certain means. The most important of these are your intentions, facing in the direction of your desired outcome, your will and your *belief* that it works. The more you want something to happen, and the clearer you can visualise the desired outcome, the stronger your will and feelings towards it will be, ensuring an avalanche of amazing people, events and circumstances will flow into your experiences, gathering speed, momentum and power as it nears your goal or dream.

The Universe (or whichever higher power you believe in) works for us and through us. Ideas are given to us but they must be carried out *through* us, in the form of asking or acting or performing a ritual or casting a specific spell. The Universe's abundance is your abundance, and it flows through your mind into manifestation. The Universe or Divine Being in which you believe, gives you the necessary ideas and clothes them with all that is needed to bring them into form when we ask *believing*.

Based on ancient human beliefs, systems and superstitions, declaring what you want and acting out your deepest desires can actually help to make things happen. Magical ideas include the notion that thought affects matter and that the trained imagination can alter the physical world, that all aspects of the

Universe are interdependent and that we can discover connections and correspondences between everyday occurrences and cosmic, or divine, energies. A miracle or a wish coming true can suggest something is going on that extends beyond the laws of nature, that something unseen has occurred; but just because we cannot see it or touch it, it doesn't mean it's not there. Magic exists, especially if you truly believe it does, but science is so far incapable of capturing its essence or the rationale behind it. Personally, I prefer to leave that task to the higher powers of the Universe.

To help your dreams come true and to use your innate power to its full effect, you can employ boosters based on the special energies and qualities of your Sun sign. These 'boosters' are chosen to be in alignment with the purpose of a particular goal, and contain energies of their own which will enhance the strength of your spell, prayer, ritual or 'asking'. Specific magical energies can be invoked by carrying out a spell or ceremony using specific herbs or colours, or on a particular day of the week, according to either your Sun sign (to heighten the power of the asking), and/or that is in sympathy with that for which you are asking (I have included days of the week for other Sun signs and spell types).

Some materials and 'boosters' you can use to increase the power, magic or energy in any area of your life include: Candles, wish lists on an appropriate piece of paper written with a specially-chosen writing tool, symbols, affirmations, chants, incense, herbs and flowers, places, colours, days of the week, elements, crystals and gemstones, animal symbols, charms, talismans, amulets, gods and goddesses, essential oils, planetary hours and your Solar totem animals. All are covered, some more briefly than others, for your very special Sun sign to radiate the energy to powerfully draw your wildest dreams towards you!

Overall, it pays to remember that the Universe (or whatever higher power/s or force/s you happen to believe in) creates *through* you that to which you give your attention. What you contemplate becomes the law of your being, and through your pure unwavering belief, is eventually brought through to manifestation on the material plane. What you think about is entirely up to you. But just be mindful that whatever you think about the most becomes your dominant thought, then your main point of attraction, and is ultimately magnified until it becomes your reality or your experience. So choose your thoughts with care. And to quote Ralph Waldo Emerson, "Be careful what you set your heart upon, for it will surely be yours." I carry a copy of this beautiful prophecy in my purse as its words resonate very strongly with me. In other words, be mindful about what you're wishing for, for you will most probably get it! Good luck!

ASTROLOGY & MAGIC

Astrology is the most sublime of the occult* sciences, while at the same time it is one of the most practical for everyday application, for it divines the human soul itself. The cosmos, particularly the patterns that formed across it at the exact moment we were born, indicates the road along which our mental and spiritual endowments are likely to impel us, therefore enabling us to prepare in advance for life's battles, pitfalls, potholes, milestones, celebrations and of course to make the utmost of opportunities. Such is the magic of the human mind, that it can 'see' into the future and relive the past without having to be physically present in either, and when combined with astrological *knowing*, particularly the knowing that springs from understanding some of the dynamics of our natal chart, however basic, our inner - and outer - magic can be lifted to phenomenal heights.

In ancient times, not only was astrology the ardent study of the most learned and powerful minds, but among the masses of ordinary people its authority and guidance accepted and followed without question. How this powerful knowledge was used was - and still is - up to the individual, but all who used it applied it to their perceived advantage.

As primitive humans observed the skies, no doubt they gradually realised that certain stars upon which their fate depended accompanied the seasons, or certain times of the year. They may also have reasoned that if governed their fate, they also governed their bodies, and it is therefore conceivable that the skies were associated with divine influence. Certain celestial influences were believed to emanate from the thirty six decans of the signs, and the mysterious but apparent effect that they exercised upon humans were thought to be due to a subtle ether shed by the heavenly stars and spheres on the Earth, that affected not only people, but also animals, plants and minerals. For the ancient mind, linking magic with astrology may have also provided a much needed sense of predictability.

Early astrologers named and made associations with the imaginary divisions of the twelve signs and the twelve houses, and people born under a certain sign were said to inherit to an extent, its properties and nature. They also believed that the influence of the planets and stars corresponded with the medicinal properties of certain plants and minerals. They therefore asserted that the influence of a star or planetary position would affect the type of medicine or healing they would offer a subject to attain the most beneficial outcome. Throughout the writings of early philosophers and theorists, there is constant reference to this unmistakable mystic connection between the seven known planets and earthly affairs and ailments. The seven metals were connected with the seven planets, to which the seven colours and the seven transformations were added. So the alchemist came to share the astrological doctrine that each planet ruled some mineral: the Sun ruled gold, the Moon silver, Mars iron, Venus copper, Saturn lead,

Jupiter tin, and Mercury quicksilver. Consequently, in alchemical symbolism the same sign came to represent the metal and its corresponding planet.

In subsequent years, astrology became closely related to alchemical knowledge and development, and the alchemist came to be regarded as an authority not only on the transmutation of metals, but also on astrology and magic. This goes some of the way to explaining how magic and divination, which had always been inseparably bound up with astrology, came to be associated with alchemy. In all the occult sciences, the supreme power was believed to be in the stars above, and from their mysterious emanations all the metals, crystals, minerals, plants and herbs derived their special properties over time. Further, as alchemy became ever more spiritual and concerned with more abstract and philosophical concepts, eventually it was considered that the transmutation of lead into gold was simply a metaphor for the transformation of base matter, in this case the human soul, into a much purer and higher state of wisdom and being.

The Sun and Moon were believed to have greater influence over the human body than all the other heavenly bodies, and to exert their influence in various ways whenever they entered a certain sign of the zodiac. And although the Moon was traditionally regarded as the most important factor of a horoscope, the Sun has come into its own in later centuries, with the result that almost everyone knows their Sun sign but only those who have delved deeper are aware of the sign their natal Moon falls in. For this reason, I have chosen to focus this book series on the twelve Sun signs, as this is what the majority of people are most familiar with.

The following pages contain methods, energies, materials and objects which may be used to increase the magic and power of your Sun sign's influence upon you. Precious stones, flowers, colours and so on, are regarded as having a potent effect upon good fortune by attuning your mind to receive harmonious vibrations from the astral forces that surround us all.

A basic working knowledge of basic astronomy and astrology is an asset when working with luck, abundance, wealth and personal power. You can attract more of these things when you align yourself with the workings of the wider Universe, the movement of the Sun, stars, Moon and planets and become aware of the correlations between the outer cycles of the skies and the inner cycles within yourself. Also, for those who are knowledgeable about Moon phases, equinoxes and solstices, a world of lucky possibilities can also magically open up to you. You don't need to know about astrology's deepest complexities to understand how everything interrelates, just learning the basics will give you an edge - and hopefully the following lucky tips will provide you with at least a small glimpse into the insights gleaned from your Sun sign, which I am certain will endow upon you the potential for amazing results to manifest in your life - and maybe even a step up one further rung towards the heavens!

* The word 'occult' comes from the Latin *occultus*, which literally means 'the knowledge of the hidden'

USING COLOURS, CRYSTALS, DEITIES, PLANTS, FOODS & MATERIAL SUBSTANCES FOR INCREASING POWER & MAGNETISING MAGIC

Material Substances are connected with abstract purposes by a complex but highly usable and accessible system of correspondences. Use these time-honoured connections in your own spells and wishes to magnetise your desires to you. The following pages will give you some materials, energies, forces and ideas you can summon the power of in order to enhance your magic and luck.

PLANETS

The Planetary influence of the day is important when 'asking' for something. If you are wishing for luck, for example, try working with your Sun Sign's inherent energies combined with the perfect day of the week for it. So an Aquarian might try using his or her natural intellect and articulate expression, to ask for greater luck on a Thursday, which is Jupiter's Day and Jupiter is renowned for being a lucky planet, or better still, ask for luck on a Saturday, which is Saturn's Day, traditional planetary ruler of Aquarius, at the time of day when Jupiter's influence is at its most powerful (information about planetary hours for each day of the week can be found on the Internet or in books on the subject, and can be complex and detailed. It is an art to memorise the correct times, days and energies for the correct spells. If you are determined enough to achieve your dream or goal however, you will be determined enough to put in the research to do it properly!) Next you will find a very simplified list of the days of the week and their meanings.

DAYS OF THE WEEK & THEIR POWERS

MONDAY ★ Moon

Cancer	The feminine, changes, emotions, secrets, dealing with women, purity, goodness, perfection, unity, psychic ability, magic, spirituality, invoking a Goddess's or angel's guidance.

TUESDAY ★ Mars

Aries & Scorpio	Enthusiasm, competition, passion, energy, courage, protection, victory,

anything requiring assertiveness, standing up for yourself, or a 'fighting spirit', determination, vitality, sexuality, self-confidence, men's power, men's mysteries, drive, ambition, achievement, triumph.

WEDNESDAY ★ Mercury

Gemini & Virgo

Education, travel, exams, study, communication, thinking, dealing with siblings, writing and speaking, knowledge, learning, adaptability, charm, youth, absorbing information.

THURSDAY ★ Jupiter

Sagittarius & Pisces

Increase (remember to be careful what you wish for), luck, growth, influence, worldly power, accomplishment, fulfilment, gambling, philosophy, higher education, abundance, optimism, expansion.

FRIDAY ★ Venus

Taurus & Libra

Love, luxury, the arts, indulgence, beauty, marriage, money, prosperity, fertility, women's power, women's mysteries, grace, charm, appeal, hope, pleasure, decorating, self-worth, self-esteem, personal values, business partnerships, romance, creativity, sharing, bonding.

SATURDAY ★ Saturn

Capricorn & Aquarius

Long-term goals, career, institutions, establishments, security, investments, karma, reversal, structure, protection, solitude, privacy, determination, ending, blocking, renewing, transforming.

SUNDAY ★ Sun

Leo

All-purpose, success, the masculine, wishes, generosity, happiness, optimism, spirit/essence, recognition, health, vitality, material wealth, invoking a God's aid or guidance, personal empowerment, spirituality.

YOUR (TRADITIONAL) PLANETARY INFLUENCE SATURN & ITS ATTRACTING POWER

FOR SERENITY, PRIVACY & SOLITUDE ★

To recharge and restore your Aquarian power after it has been depleted by your often frenetic activity and over-thinking!

Planet: Saturn

Colours: Black, brown, dark blue

Scents/Incense: Myrrh, geranium, lavender, jasmine, patchouli, sandalwood

Gems/Crystals: Sodalite, geodes

Plants/Herbs/Spices: Yew, chamomile, passionflower, lemon balm, lavender, ashwagandha

Gods/Goddesses/'Guides': Lares, Buddha, Forseti, Kuthumi, Babaji, Lakshmi, Saint Francis, Serapis Bey, Maitreya, Yogananda

Miscellaneous symbolism: A cave-dwelling hibernating bear, or similarly solitary wild animals, serene nature images

FOR SUCCESSFUL STUDY ★ To keep that brilliant Aquarian mind sparkling and fresh!

Planets: Saturn, Jupiter, Uranus

Colours: Red, purple, blue

Scents/Incense: Rosemary, basil, juniper, peppermint, clary sage

Gems/Crystals: Mangano Calcite, fluorite

Plants/Herbs/Spices: Saffron, ginseng, peppermint, rosemary, basil, black tea, green tea, periwinkle, sage

Gods/Goddesses/'Guides': Archangel Uriel, Archangel Zadkiel, Kali, Kuthumi, Saint-Germain

Miscellaneous symbolism: Old high ceiling, multi-level bookshelf libraries, mortarboard (graduation hat)

FOR PROTECTION ★ To protect and enhance your greatest asset - your mind - and its requirement of you to be present here in the *now* - not somewhere too far ahead in the future! Also, to protect you from hindering or negative influences.

Planets: Mars & Saturn

Colours: Black, brown, dark blue, dark green, white, blue

Scents/Incense: Myrrh, patchouli

Gems/Crystals: Red tourmaline, black tourmaline, topaz, garnet, amber, green aventurine, turquoise, aquamarine, carnelian

Plants/Herbs/Spices: Cactus, basil, primrose, marigold, rowan, holly, bay, hyacinth, geranium, hawthorn, chrysanthemum

Gods/Goddesses/'Guides': Athena, Mars, Saturn, Tara, Kali, Ashtar, Cernunnos, Artemis, Archangel Michael

Miscellaneous symbolism: Guardian angels, Eye of Ra, Algiz (Rune stone), Nazur Boncugu

YOUR NATAL MOON PHASE

Although this book is aimed at enhancing your life through the energy of your Sun sign, a bit of lunar help can give your wishing a boost. As well as using the planetary days and hours system to make your wishes, try combining your Sun sign's power periods with your natal Moon phase (your natal Moon phase can be calculated using a number of sources on the internet, or through an astrologer), or even studying which constellation the Moon is situated in at certain times, to increase the power of your spells and asking rituals. For example, you might like to 'ask' for a promotion at work during a New/Waxing Moon period, particularly if the Moon happens to fall under an auspicious sign for career advancement, such as Capricorn. Your natal Moon phase can also be used to similar effect, by researching when your Moon phase will coincide with a certain lunar constellation position.

For many centuries, people across the world have recognised that the Moon influences the affairs of all living things on planet Earth. The waxing Moon appears to have a drawing, increasing and enhancing effect, whereas the waning Moon has a decreasing, receding and withdrawing effect. All things that come into being are stamped with the qualities of the prevailing Moon stage. It seems that people born during certain lunar phases tend to share specific attributes with other people born during this same phase. In turn, their attributes will be subtly different from those of individuals born during any of the other stages in the Moon cycle. Knowing exactly which phase of the Moon you were born under gives you all kinds of extraordinarily valuable insights into your character, emotions, behaviour and motivation in life. It can make you aware of your deepest underlying drives, the fundamental purpose that you are drawn towards in life and the contribution you can make to others and society during the course of your lifetime. This knowledge may enable you to intuit and make the most of your own personal cyclical pattern that you go through each month, and allow you to know when the most auspicious periods of time are for you and your affairs, nurture yourself and channel your energies in the most positive directions.

Because this lunar pattern repeats itself every month, you will find that you can also pace yourself on a long-term basis. This will enable you to effectively target your efforts and goals on periods of time that you know will be potentially fortunate for you. You may in fact find that your birth phase corresponds with the days of the month when you have abundant energy, feel inspired and can generate new ideas with ease. During this period you should work towards the fruition of your efforts, bring your dreams into light and reach for the stars!

The Lunar Phases Are:

★ New Moon

★ First/Waxing Crescent

★ First Quarter

★ Waxing Gibbous Moon

★ Full Moon

★ Waning Gibbous / Disseminating Moon

★ Last Quarter

★ Waning Crescent / Balsamic Moon

★ Back to the New Moon

SPELLS, MAGIC & WISHING WITH MOON PHASES

Depending on what sort of spell you wish to perform, your spell will take place during the waxing, full or waning cycle of the Moon. Each phase of the

Moon is good for some types of magic, but not so much for others.

NEW MOON (WAXING) GOING FROM NEW TO FULL

An exceptional time to work magic and make wishes for new beginnings, and for the conception and initiation of new projects. The Waxing Moon is appropriate for spells, rituals and workings that involve growth, healing and increase. This is a period of time lasting approximately two weeks, to draw things toward you and increase things, such as love, prosperity and new opportunities. During this period is the time to bless new projects, anything that requires energy to grow, such as gardens, business ventures, new homes, or educational pursuits. Personal growth and healing are accented, as is 'attraction magic' - drawing something to you such as love, abundance, health, success or a new path - and if done well, you can expect results by the next Full Moon. Magical workings for gain, increase or bringing things to you should be initiated when the Moon is waxing (or New, going from Dark to Full). A time for divination of all kinds, spells of spiritual intention, and for any creative project you wish to see birthed, with magical and fruitful results.

While making a wish within the first forty-eight hours after the New Moon is a powerful way of helping it come to fruition, the most potent time for making wishes is actually within the first eight hours of the exact time of its position. Write down your wish list within this first eight hours on a piece of appropriately coloured paper with a special writing tool, and be sure to capture the essence of your wish by wording it in a way that charges your emotions and simply feels 'right'. Make a maximum of ten wishes (less is perfectly fine too), as making too many wishes might disperse their energy too much to be effective. After writing down your list and releasing your wishes to the Universe in whichever form you feel happy with, keep your list and check on it in a few days', weeks' or months' time to assess whether anything has shifted in the direction of your listed dreams, desires or goals. I'll bet it has - or at the very least, something even better has arrived in its place!

While the New Moon is not known as a time for 'banishing' or releasing things we no longer want in our lives, I feel that if we are to ask and wish for things, we need to make room to receive them. Making room means that the Universe can slot it right into our lives where we have cleared our paths for it. Clutter, unwanted things, possessions that no longer serve us, are all things we can banish. Taurean energy can give us the tendency to hold on to possessions, hoard things, be greedy, get stuck in a rut, be stubborn about letting go, and accumulate too much material 'stuff'. So, to help what you are asking for come into your life quicker, the New Moon is a particularly opportune time to throw a few things out so you can make way for the new and clear up some space for that which you are wishing for. What are you waiting for? Start creating a space for your wishes today!

FULL MOON

The highest energy occurs at the Full Moon and therefore this is a powerful time for magical workings. This phase lasts approximately 3 days, 24 hours before the exact Full Moon, the day of, and 24 hours after it, giving us 3 full days to perform our spells. However, we are not strictly limited to a three-day period; the power of this phase can actually be accessed for seven days - three days prior to, the night of, and the three days after the Full Moon. The Full Moon period is when the Moon is at her most powerful, being the most luminous and radiant part of the cycle. Known as the 'high tide' of psychic power, the Full Moon represents culmination, climax, fulfilment and abundance. The Full Moon governs all kinds of magic, including manifestation, banishing, and is particularly good for calling forth protection and heightening your intuitive abilities. The Full Moon contains magic that calls forth personal power, protection, fertility, spiritual development, and psychic awareness. Cleansing of ritual tools, crystals, wish lists, Tarot decks, and the like can be done now. Magic worked during the Full Moon often takes one complete cycle to come to fruition. Try also reaffirming your desires during the New Moon to give them an added nudge in the right direction.

WANING MOON

The Waning Moon represents the lunar cycle from Full to Dark. Any spells and magic performed during this period is based purely around banishing and releasing. It could involve releasing things which no longer serve you, banishing negative energies, and removing obstacles which are standing in the way of achieving your goals or dreams. The Waning Moon is the best time for cleansing, gently releasing, eliminating, expelling and completion. It is of great assistance when you are wanting to let go of something, or someone, gradually. The Dark of the Moon, the period when the Moon is no longer visible to the naked eye, until the New Moon, is the most useful time for divination of all kinds.

★ What is your natal Moon phase type? Can you think of ways you can combine it with the power of your Sun sign to effect change and bring about wonderful happenings? ★

THE MOON & WHAT IT REPRESENTS IN THE HUMAN PSYCHE & NATAL CHART

The Moon in the sky shines with the reflected light of the Sun. Although not a planet, the Moon is our nearest celestial neighbour and exerts a great influence upon us. The gravitational pull of the Moon affects our body fluids, which contribute to about 90 per cent of our biological make-up. It moves at approximately half a degree per hour and takes an average of 27.3 days to pass through all twelve zodiac signs, staying in each for around 2.5 days.

In astrology the Moon corresponds with the way in which we reflect and respond to what is going on around us. It has to do with our feelings, emotions and instincts and, in the same way the Moon influences the tides on planet Earth, it symbolises the ebb and flow of our emotional nature, our moods, fluctuations and changeability. The Moon is the archetype of the Mother, which is within us all, and represents the primary feminine principle in the natal chart. It is through the Moon that we express our parental instincts - caring, nurturing, protecting, sensitivity. The Moon has links with the past and the subconscious and it is from this almost primitive source that our natural instinctual forces flow.

The Moon is essentially a feminine principle and associates with the inner personality, receptivity, passivity and inward-oriented feelings. It can act as an inner guide to the deeper self, the unconscious self, figures half-shrouded in mystery, linking the hidden personal world of the subconscious to the clearer world of personal awareness.

The Moon is the innermost core of our being, private feelings, habitual reactions and subconscious habits. It is the caring, nurturing sustainer of life, the 'mother' of the zodiac. It tells us about how we seek security, our urge to nurture, our nurturing style, our responses and feelings and moods. The innermost core of our being, private feelings, subconscious habits. It is concerned with habits, mothering, habitual/instinctive responses and personality. It is our karma, our soul, our past.

The Moon represents our mother or mother figure, our feminine side, maternal instinct, our nurturing style and needs, our unconscious self, our emotional reactions, the subconscious, our feelings, instincts, intuition, receptivity, habits, what we need to feel secure, fluctuations, cycles, moods, and our childhood.

> The Moon is essentially receptive and passive; it reflects the life experience rather than initiating it. Fluctuating and cyclical, the Moon is the planet (although technically a satellite) of the childhood experience, and instinctual reactions. It represents the mother (a child's experience and expectations of their mother), maternal instincts and the feminine principle, indicating how strongly these manifest in an individual, male or female.

As it represents what our childhood experience is likely to be, and childhood is essentially a time where our consciousness has not yet fully developed, our Moon sign traits seem to be more apparent in our younger years. We will usually show our Moon sign traits more so than our Sun sign traits during this developing period of infancy and early childhood, until we have the presence of mind to more consciously develop our ego and true core self (the Sun).

> The symbol for the Moon ☽ is a representation of its crescent in its waxing phase from new to full, but it can also be seen as two half circles - these form a bowl shape, a receptacle, a feminine container that 'receives' and 'holds' anything put into it. The half circle, unlike the full circle of the Sun, is finite and incomplete, almost as if striving for wholeness.

The Moon represents our *soul*.

YOUR MOON SIGN

Your Moon Sign, representing your soul, and your Sun sign, representing your spirit, work together to form the foundation of your basic personality, expression and nature. If you know what your Moon sign is, look it up below and read how it works with your Aquarian Sun to blend your mind, soul and spirit.

♈ With the Moon in ARIES, Sun in Aquarius, you are likely to be ★ Observant, astute, self-interested, alert, emotionally detached, enthusiastic, independent, honest, devoted to truth, loyal, adventurous, hot-tempered, independent, courageous, prophetic, overly assertive, temperamental, insensitive, ambitious, self-reliant, energetic, emotionally bold and reckless, restless, speak before thinking, a fast communicator, soundly intellectual, acid-tongued, respectful of others' opinions, pioneering, original, forward-looking, lively, witty, frank, bright, of-the-wall, rebellious, an intelligent individualist, one who has moral integrity, and a maverick truth-seeker.

Sun/Moon Harmony Rating ★ 8 out of 10

♉ With the Moon in TAURUS, Sun in Aquarius, you are likely to be ★ Calm, level-headed, pragmatically intellectual, easygoing, possessive, stubborn, materialistic, gentle, infinitely patient, slow and steady-paced, conflicted between security and freedom, tenacious, emotionally placid, devoted to causes, reluctant to listen to others' views if convinced your own are correct, logical and detached in emotional matters, stoic, faithful, friendly, capable, determined, resourceful, dependable, an eccentric entrepreneur, ambitious, peace-loving but strong-willed, reliable, philanthropic, thoughtful, realistic, sensible, persistent, and dedicated to grounding your inspiration and idealism.

Sun/Moon Harmony Rating ★ 5 out of 10

♊ With the Moon in GEMINI, Sun in Aquarius, you are likely to be ★ A free spirit, changeable, friendly, bright, breezy, emotionally versatile, quick-witted, philosophical but flippant, perceptive, clever, inspiring, stimulating, sociable, detached, flexible yet stubborn, iconoclastic, curious, emotionally impulsive, restless, easily bored, logical, creative, progressive, communicative, strongly socially aware, unsentimental, emotionally naïve, gifted, a wonderful friend, original, popular, funny, easily swept away by ideas and concepts, open towards and perceptive of new ideas, idealistic, intellectual, squandering of your natural talents, reluctant to face the darker aspects of life, too busy to deal with feelings, and ruled by your mind rather than your gut instincts. **

Sun/Moon Harmony Rating ★ 9 out of 10

♋ With the Moon in CANCER, Sun in Aquarius, you are likely to be ★ Passive, sensitive, intuitive, emotionally expressive, strongly socially conscious, compassionate, a kind-hearted rebel, sympathetic, shy, emotionally reticent, hidden, private, eccentric, peaceful, imaginative, poetic, intelligently kind, devoted to truth and the triumph of the human spirit, helpful, companionable, emotionally lofty, progressive but old-fashioned values, able to express universal insights through personal projection, a sensitive individualist, self-protective, unconsciously prejudiced, likely to become absorbed with abstract causes which cuts you off from your feelings, and occasionally moved to emotional outbursts.

Sun/Moon Harmony Rating ★ 5 out of 10

♌ With the Moon in LEO, Sun in Aquarius, you are likely to be ★ Proud, independent, individualistic, gentle on the surface with a great strength within, dramatic, a fearless defender of principles and causes, artistic, wise and generous in helping others, visionary, passionate, radiantly humanitarian, enthusiastic for new and original ideas, trustworthy, a good leader of groups, romantically imaginative, open, charismatic, powerful, extroverted, honest, passionate, warm, bold, inclined to get carried away by romance and idealism and forget to return to earth, direct, vain, glamorising of others and failing to see their true colours, friendly, stubbornly controlling, generous, expressive, ambitious, despotic, self-centred, self-reliant, creative, emotionally radiating warmth, emotionally idealistic, luxury-loving, helpful, demonstrative, and creatively imaginative.

Sun/Moon Harmony Rating ★ 7 out of 10

♍ With the Moon in VIRGO, Sun in Aquarius, you are likely to be ★ Puritanical, intelligent, judgemental, cool, calm and collected, aloof, critical, clever, discriminating, an emotional perfectionist, methodical, studious, a devoted researcher, helpful, a truth-seeker, serious, kind-hearted, innovative, mentally alert, unassuming, mentally dextrous, efficient, undemonstrative, caring, rigid, reserved, rebellious yet conventional, objectively rational, cool-headed, willing to help and do what needs to be done, altruistic, genuinely kind, bright, devoted to ideals, dry-witted, and radical yet uptight.

Sun/Moon Harmony Rating ★ 6 out of 10

♎ With the Moon in LIBRA, Sun in Aquarius, you are likely to be ★ Lively, intellectual, able to work with principles easily, see life from endlessly new vantage points, sociable, refined, paradoxical, generally well-balanced and moderate, easygoing, sporadically affectionate, popular, a hider of feelings, graceful, charming, approachable, tolerant, distanced from your true emotional power, accessible, civilised, sharing, gracious, cooperative, approval-seeking, hospitable, hedonistic, indecisive, interested in people, places and purposes globally, romantically idealistic, endearing, acutely observant, loving of people, quick witted, honest, refined, shocking and delightful at the same time, colourfully persuasive, artistically sensitive, abstract, emotionally naïve, and

conflicted between independence and needing others.
**

Sun/Moon Harmony Rating ★ 9 out of 10

♏ With the Moon in SCORPIO, Sun in Aquarius, you are likely to be ★ Intense, powerfully intellectual, forceful, highly charged, extreme and radical, possessive, keenly insightful, investigative, unbending, strong-willed, self-judging, a reformer, dominating, intensely dedicated to ideals, passionate, unyielding, resourceful, resilient, controlling, stubborn, persevering and thorough, devoted to truth at any cost, fiercely principled, psychologically penetrative, secretive, passionate yet dispassionate, loyal, emotional, courageously dedicated to reform and improvement for the welfare of others, an astute observer, perceptive, self-reliant, dogmatic, stern, exacting, potentially ruthless and manipulative, and emotionally powerful.

Sun/Moon Harmony Rating ★ 6 out of 10

♐ With the Moon in SAGITTARIUS, Sun in Aquarius, you are likely to be ★ Eager, adventurous, friendly, independent, idealistic, a traveller of body and mind, big-hearted, honest, adventurous, rationalising, impatient with petty details and restrictions of daily life, prone to preach when advancing causes, unaware of the subtleties of social intercourse, intellectual, inquisitive, an adventurer, able to see the 'big picture', idealistic, distant from your feelings, emotionally reckless, a free spirit, non-committal, a good teacher, in possession of a zany sense of humour, far-sighted, intellectually speedy, independent, optimistic, a lover of learning, inspiring, outrageous, aspiring, gregarious, socially concerned, broad-minded, rebellious, expansive, verbose, emotionally philosophical, freedom-seeking, and guided by reason rather than emotion.

Sun/Moon Harmony Rating ★ 9 out of 10

♑ With the Moon in CAPRICORN, Sun in Aquarius, you are likely to be ★ Dependable, steadfast, resourceful, committed to causes, independent, driven to succeed, ambitious to make the world a better place, critical, reserved, withdrawn, cool, unemotional, wise, shrewd, organised, down-to-earth, efficient, reliable, serious, sensible, materialistic, introverted, understanding of practical applications and wisdom, economical, brotherly, a practical reformer, 'a rebel with a cause', inventive, personally honourable, overly-strict when adhering to principles, fearlessness, uptight, socially rigid, self-contained, aware of human character, sardonically humorous, and willing to work in the present for the future good.

Sun/Moon Harmony Rating ★ 6.5 out of 10

♒ With the Moon in AQUARIUS, Sun in Aquarius, you are likely to be ★ Friendly and tolerant, independent, idealistic, emotionally detached, eccentric, 'different', unconventional, aloof, paradoxical, imaginative, sympathetic, unconventional, honest, original, forward-moving, inventive, impersonal in relationships, clear-headed, highly observant, acutely aware of the human condition, progressive, scientifically oriented, objective, living an unusual lifestyle in some way, well-meaning, open to the unusual, emotionally naïve, over-identifying with causes, blunt and insensitive when comparing people with your ideals, freedom-loving, unorthodox, idealistic, impractical, loyal, humanitarian, globally aware, courageous and committed to your ideals, a law unto yourself, and in possession of an eternal sense of hope and belief in human potential.

Sun/Moon Harmony Rating ★ 8 out of 10

♓ With the Moon in PISCES, Sun in Aquarius, you are likely to be ★ Highly imaginative, intuitive, with the ability to blend common sense and mysticism, over-idealistic, a chaser of spiritual rainbows, heart in the right place, good-natured, intriguing, kindly, friendly, emotionally intelligent, apt to wander off on your own and go into flights of fancy, hot and cold emotions, sentimental, gentle, accepting, intuitive, understanding, independent but vulnerable, a thinker and a poet, altruistic, in possession of a universal outlook, humorous, psychologically insightful, generous, receptive, creative, reverent, forgiving, devoutly committed to social causes, mysterious, empathetic, humanitarian, prone to drifting and wasting time in daydreams, impressionable, idealistic but easily swayed, gullible, impractical, evasive, sensitive, psychic, perceptive, emotionally intelligent, able to mix and work with all types of people, and aware of the needs of others.

Sun/Moon Harmony Rating ★ 8 out of 10

** If your Moon is in Gemini or Libra, your Sun and Moon will form what is known in astrology as a trine aspect. This aspect is the easiest, most flowing and harmonious astrological aspect, ensuring that your Sun and Moon, or spirit and soul, are well integrated. With both luminaries in Air signs, this gives them the best possible degree of complementary energy - a blending of the elements suggests a balanced expression of personality. One drawback of the trine aspect lies in the fact that its easy flow can be *too* harmonious; if our path is too smooth and difficulties don't arise to challenge us from time to time, we can often become lazy and complacent, stunting our growth and spiritual evolution. As Air signs, you share the art of sociability, are highly idealistic, affable, romantic, possess a good intellect, have a love of truth and beauty, are reasonable, broad-minded, independent but devoted to your ideals, have an artistic sensitivity, are tolerant, understanding, civilised and dignified, and have avant-garde tastes, but may be detached, cool, head over heart-oriented, and restless.

YOUR BODY & HEALTH

Aquarians are among the longest-lived types of the zodiac. Your constitution is wiry rather than strong and although you are quite willing to engage in physical toil if you have to, you're not really built for stamina or prolonged exertion. Aquarius is associated with the Calves, Lower Legs, Ankles, Circulation and Spinal Cord. Aquarians need lots of fresh air, sleep and regular exercise to stay healthy. You have tremendous reserves of nervous energy, and it is this rather than physical vitality that keeps you going at such a rate. When you have an idea or an ideal to work towards, you have the capacity for intense effort for lengthy periods - but your mental interest must be absorbed. You also need your friends around you; companionship is like a therapy to you whenever you feel jaded or depleted, and if you are denied this connection with a wide variety of people, you are likely to start to feel under par. Yet you also require very definite periods of seclusion, to relax in solitude or wander off alone into a forest to restore your mind, body and spirit. Your dynamism and volatile energies will quickly replenish if you do take this necessary time out when you need it. Often your manic mental activity can manifest as nervous complaints and stress-related conditions, which usually sort themselves out without much fuss, but the Water Bearer may develop phobias.

Aquarius seems to suffer according to the weather conditions - which are always too hot, too cold, too humid, or too dry. Circulatory problems and diseases of the blood and nervous system are common in Aquarians, and they are prone to varicose veins, and calf and ankle accidents or afflictions. There is also a connection with the heart through your opposite sign Leo, making you prone in later life to suffering from hardening of the arteries. This isn't usually a problem for too many Aquarians however, as you generally tend to live a moderate, temperate kind of lifestyle.

As Aquarius is linked with the sudden and unexpected energy of the planet Uranus, they may suffer from unpredictable, inexplicable illnesses that can then clear up again just as mysteriously. As

Uranus governs cerebral and nervous functions, rhythmic systems, spasms, the ankles, and circulation, these areas of your body may also need to be kept in check. Uranus is also associated with fractures, and if these occur, they usually strike below the knee. Uranus is also said to rule those parts of the eye which, when developed, can see the human aura. Furthermore, it has a marked influence over the nervous system, especially over the electrical impulses which pass between the nerve cells.

Keeping yourself in excellent health overall, with a special awareness, of Aquarius's vulnerable points, is key to achieving all you set out to do, and getting the most out of your life!

THE CELL SALTS ★ ASTROLOGICAL TONICS

Homeopathy and astrology have colluded to provide a wonderful list of astrological tonics, one particularly suited to each of the twelve signs. These are called 'homeopathic cell salts', 'tissue salts' or 'biochemic cell salts', and are available in most health food stores, are inexpensive and easy to take. They are considered to be gentle, effective and safe, even for children, people in fragile health states, and the elderly. Although the full picture, drawn from a full natal horoscope, gives a fuller, more accurate idea of an individual's unique constitution, even simply working with one's date of birth can be enough for the medical astrologer to suggest the use of a cell salt based upon the correlation with their Sun sign. As well as the cell salts having a significant effect upon physical ailments, they can also profoundly influence the subtle energy bodies, including the mental, emotional, etheric and spiritual. Although, the most common use of these salts is based upon correspondence with a Sun sign, use of the cell salt related to one's Moon sign can assist with addressing deeper underlying emotional issues, such as anxiety, depression, panic and fear. Indeed, in the first seven years of life, when the Moon is the most influential planet, the lunar cell salts are the most appropriate choice as a tonic. For the purposes of this book, however, I will outline the cell salts that correlate with your Sun sign only.

TISSUE SALT FOR AQUARIUS ★ NAT MUR.

Nat mur. (Natrum muriaticum) is the cell salt for Aquarius. Nat mur. has the effect of regulating fluids by attracting or drawing away water from affected parts of the body, to redistribute it wherever it is needed. Aquarius rules the circulation and blood, the ankles, the spinal cord and the electrical impulses of the nerves, and Nat mur. may help in supporting the smooth and even flow of electricity through and across the nerves. Symptoms of insufficient Nat mur. are insomnia, improper or dysfunctional nerve synapse firing, intermittent nerve pains, dry skin conditions, eczema, digestive complaints, dryness or excessive salivation in the mouth, watery colds, constipation or herpes and/or blisters on or around the mucus membranes. Nat mur. is otherwise known as sodium chloride, or table salt, and overall it is said to be good at regulating the water supply throughout the body, therefore affecting elimination and how cold or hot we feel regardless of the temperature.

MONEY ATTRIBUTES

Colour for Increased Earning Power ★ Aqua

Aquarian writer W. Somerset Maugham once said, "Money is like a sixth sense without which you cannot make a complete use of the other five." He also quoted, "Money is the string with which a sardonic destiny directs the motions of its puppets." These statements reveal much about the Water Bearer's financial nature. It is a rare Aquarian who pursues money for its own sake. You may be shrewd, clever, successful and even have expensive tastes, but you are not avaricious. To you, money is indeed the sixth sense. You tend to take financial gain for granted, as it always seems to be there when you need it, and it flows naturally when you are doing the right thing, trusting your instincts and acting on hunches and inspired ideas.

Aquarians are either frugal or impulsive in their spending habits, depending on which planetary ruler is strongest. If Saturn is strong, you are tight-fisted and careful, knowing to the cent how much money you have. If Uranus is strong, your financial world is usually in chaos, fuelled by mounting debts and unusual business schemes. Aquarians are generally not spendthrifts however, caring more for ideals than for material possessions, and you are intelligent enough to discern what is a wise investment and what is not. Your innate futuristic thinking can make you have almost prophetic visions about your future financial standing, which you should tap into, to your advantage. Your instincts are usually excellent, scrupulous even, as are your potential money-making abilities - and both will work best when you're not even trying. Just like you don't make a conscious effort to be intuitive, money will similarly just arrive as a side-effect of trying to accomplish another aim altogether. Therefore, it would do you well to explore the possibility of doing professionally an aspect of what you are already doing voluntarily. This brings me to the next point of the Aquarian financial nature: that of compassion and generosity, which comes naturally to you, but can sometimes get the better of you. Many Aquarians are charitable and philanthropic, due to their aim to achieve a better lot for all, but these laudable qualities can also place an enormous burden on your resources and monetary status.

Security is of less concern to the Water Bearer than freedom; and indeed, money buys you freedom and independence, which enable you to live the life you please. You may create money through inventions, your unique talents, or genius ideas that no one else has thought of. A brilliant invention or unique concept, borne out of your innate desire to improve mankind, could well make your fortune. Aquarians, more so than any other Sun sign, have fine talents and often have incipient genius lying latent and undeveloped in their subconscious, and unfortunately it may only be on rare occasions that these are ever called to the surface. Many Aquarians, apparently quite ordinary and undistinguished, might rise to a high place in the world if they would but apply themselves to developing these hidden powers. Self-confidence, overcoming your fixed obstinacy, recognition of worthwhile ideas, and the ability to share and generate those ideas, are needed to pull it off.

COLOURS

We vibrate to the frequency of colour, shown through its continual movement and change in our aura. One of the most beautiful examples of colour is the rainbow. This architect of colour is caused by the refraction and internal reflection of light in raindrops. Colour can be perceived as either a pigment, or as illumination. The colour spectrum can be divided into eight main colours: red, orange, yellow, green, turquoise, blue, violet and magenta. Each of these has its own frequency and wavelength and because of this, coupled with the fact that we as living energy centres emanate colour, colour can be a great medium in healing, calming, energising, increasing and attracting.

Each Sun sign has a specific colour or colours which when used in combination with wishing rituals, can enhance their power immensely. Coloured candles can be used to good effect, as the fire energy of the flame/s increases the power of any wish, and flames are also a useful aid to meditating on, focusing upon or clarifying what you want. Coloured candles help to focus the energy for whatever purpose the colour is in sympathy with (e.g. green for money, pink for romance, red for confidence, etc.) Wearing your Sun sign's magical colour/s on a regular basis will also bring great benefits.

YOUR LUCKY COLOURS

For Aquarius ★ Electric blue, turquoise, sky blue, electric green, violet, purple, deep amethyst

For Uranus ★ Light blue, silvery white, fluorescent colours, cobalt blue, shocking pink, electric and glaring hues, and stripes and swirls of many colours

Each of the eight colours of the rainbow spectrum also has a complementary colour to which it is matched. Red is complementary to turquoise, orange to blue, yellow to violet, and green to magenta. If these colour pairs enhance each other's most spellbinding qualities and energies, perhaps you could try wearing your Sun sign's lucky colour with its matching complementary colour in order to produce extra magical results! Your lucky Aquarian colour is turquoise, which complements red. Now you know your colours, you can dress for success!

FEATURE COLOURS ★ ELECTRIC BLUE & TURQUOISE

Meanings ★ A steely, brilliant light blue, electric blue has a vivid magnificence that is awe-inspiring and pleasing to the eye. It is a wondrous version of the colour blue, and can also resemble the shade of turquoise, in a heightened, more luminous form. The colour blue symbolises inspiration, devotion, peace and tranquillity. It is calming and is an excellent healing colour. Blue also creates a sense of space, so any room or area painted in this colour will appear larger. Because of its calming vibes, it is a soothing and useful colour with which to treat headaches, tension, stress and insomnia.

Turquoise is a variation of the colour blue, and is derived by mixing together blue and green. It can veer towards either of these colours but is best known as possessing a vibrant, opaque bright bluish tone. It indicates a dynamic quality of being, a highly energised personality, positive influence over others, and the ability to project oneself to beneficial effect -

great for getting those brilliant ideas across! Turquoise is a wonderful all-round healer and general tonic for the immune system.

Overall, blue, and particularly electric blue, cobalt blue and turquoise, are Aquarius's special POWER colours!

LUCKY CAREER TIPS & PATHS THAT WILL MAKE YOUR BANK BALANCE & SPIRITUAL SELF SOAR

With your Sun in Aquarius, you are inventive, original and have a systematic way of thinking. Computers, modern technology, and anything new or cutting edge and mentally challenging will attract you. Being a humanitarian and revolutionary at heart, alternative healing paths (especially within groups or communities) and social groups and issues will also appeal, for you love to effect societal change. In no way could you be described as conventional, so it is natural that many Aquarians choose a career which is different, unorthodox, unexpected, or embraces the unusual or alternative. This is the sign of inventors, scientists, social workers, brilliant thinkers, humanists, occultists, political reformers and revolutionaries. Alternative therapies, gadgets, coming up with new and innovative ideas, or working for political reform, are all hobbies which often develop into careers. Your ideal vocation allows you freedom, independence, autonomy, occasionally working within groups and to invent new systems which benefit society.

For the more Saturnian or conventional Aquarians, the following fields may hold appeal: Aviation, Counselling, Electrics and Electronics, Radar, Sonar or Television, Photography, Research, Selling Unusual Antiques or Books, Specialist Hobbies or Social Clubs.

Ideal careers for Aquarius overall are: Scientist, Astrologer, Inventor, Radiologist, Art Dealer, Television Broadcaster, Ecologist, Human Rights Officer, Protestor, Radical Healer, Magician, Laser Technician, Recording Studio Engineer, Telecommunications Worker, Social Worker, New Age Healer, Aid Worker, Politician, Laboratory Technician, Sociologist, Aeronautic Worker, Aviator, Broadcaster, Faith Healer, New Age Teacher, Nuclear Physicist, Science and Space Technologist, Alternative Health Worker or Self-Development Guru. Many of these professions reflect the fact that Aquarians are ahead of their time.

Of course this does not account for everyone born under the sign of the Water Bearer, but for those of you who are strongly in tune with your ruling planet Uranus, there is certainly an element of the 'avant garde' in your nature and you don't fit the standard, conventional mould. Essentially, Uranus rules astrologers, anything to do with electricity, natural and social scientists, aviators, inventors, numerologists, and those delving into the occult sciences in general. Its influence is most pronounced in all aspects of computer programming and technology, space science, and concepts in futuristic and/or technological advancement. Some purely Uranian types will be fiercely self-sufficient and radical nonconformists who prefer to blaze new trails, challenge the status quo, alter the world for the better, and experiment with new progressive ideas or methods, carving for themselves a deeply life-changing and original career as they go - and might even reinvent themselves into eccentric millionaires in the meantime!

AIR SIGN AQUARIUS & THE SANGUINE HUMOR

Greek historian Hippocrates (460 - 370 BC) theorised that certain human behaviours were caused by body fluids (called 'humors'). Then Galen of Pergamon (AD 131 - 200), a Greek physician, developed the first typology of temperaments to encompass many facets of the human psyche and physiology. These also related to the classical elements of fire, earth, air and water - as choleric, melancholic, sanguine and phlegmatic respectively.

The Air element corresponds with the humor Sanguine, which is characterised by quick, impulsive and relatively short-lived reactions. Sanguine types are driven by the need for attention and acceptance, social contact, relating, relationships, and trying to impress others. A Sanguine disposition represents positivity, optimism, extroversion, openness, expressiveness, talkativeness, light-heartedness, and sociability. It is associated with hot and moist conditions.

LUCKY PLACES WHERE YOUR ENERGY IS HEIGHTENED

As the Air element and Sanguine humor corresponds with hot and moist conditions, warm, humid, tropical places suit your constitution, disposition and temperament. The following nations and cities are also places whose vibrations are closely allied with the sign of Aquarius: Ethiopia, Italy (Trent), Prussia, Lithuania, Canada, Germany (Bremen, Hamburg), Sweden (Stockholm), Austria (Salzburg), Russia (Leningrad, St Petersburg, Moscow, Siberia), Cyprus and Scandinavia. Israel, Iran, Abyssinia, North America (Los Angeles) and some parts of Arabia and Poland, are also in tune with the Aquarian energy, as are hippie trails, communes, and offbeat and unusual places. A group adventure to the ski slopes or a palm-tree fringed tropical island paradise upon which a hippie retreat or commune exists, could very well be your ticket to Aquarian heaven!

GEMS & CRYSTALS

Crystals act as 'transmitters' and 'amplifiers' of your will or intentions - as long as your will or intentions are in sympathy with the crystal's energy. The mineral kingdom refers to stones, minerals and crystals and the associations and vibrations they carry. When working with stones, we are working with several different layers of spiritual energies, and although they can be regarded as inanimate 'psychic batteries', they are actually moving, vibrating masses of energy which transmit potential and power into our lives. Some crystals and stones even have receptive powers, which means they can absorb energy and retain it within until cleansed.

Although it is untrue that the only stones you can usefully wear are the ones astrologically matched with your Sun sign or ruling planet, those which align with your Sun sign or ruling planet are the most fortuitous and appropriate 'attractors' and 'amplifiers'.

However, nobody is under the rule of one planet alone. We are all in essence a complex mixture of every planet, many elements and varying aspects, depending on their positions, placements and prominence in our birth chart. Everything that goes on in the skies above us affects what is going on here on Earth, and also *within* us. Your lucky stones are to assist you to tune into your Sun sign's energy and planetary influences, but you are by no means limited to the ones listed for your sign alone. Above all, let your stones, whichever ones you choose, work for you and allow them to transport your very own unique and magical energy into the wider Universe.

AQUARIAN & URANIAN LUCKY CRYSTALS, STONES & GEMS

Amethyst, garnet, aquamarine (your three primary birthstones), zircon, jacinth (Uranus), and jargoon (Uranus), are your luckiest stones, and one or more of these gems should be worn about your person to ensure good luck and increase your magnetism. Magnetite, sugilite, tourmaline, dermantine, apatite, jade, diamond, bixbyite, blue obsidian, blue sapphire, chrysoprase, blue celestite, fuchsite, Boji stone, black pearl, slate, hematite, cavansite, amber (Uranus), angelite, blue lace agate, labradorite, cavansite, clear quartz, moonstone, imperial topaz, fluorite, antacamite, larimar and turquoise also align with Aquarius's energy.

FEATURE CRYSTAL ★ AMETHYST

'The Spiritual and Psychic Stone'

An extremely well-known, common, easy-to-find and popular stone, this is the stone of spiritual power and psychic energy. It has a high spiritual vibration and is an extremely powerful and protective stone, particularly for those born under the sign of Aquarius and Pisces. It awakens and activates our higher awareness and psychic abilities. Amethyst has strong cleansing and healing powers, and its serenity assists with enhancing meditation and reaching higher states of consciousness. Connected with the Crown and Third Eye chakras, amethyst offers protection, wisdom, focus, power, divine understanding, ethereal awareness, psychic abilities, healing and inner peace. Its best known use is for heightening and enhancing one's spiritual connections and insights; it can even open doors to other dimensions and realities. It is calming, balancing and comforting, and helpful with easing stress-related insomnia. Amethyst can be worn on parts of the upper body to encourage conversations with your higher self, and is especially beneficial worn over the throat or heart. Encouraging selflessness, intuition, spiritual wisdom and divine visualisation, amethyst can transmute earthly energies to the higher vibrations of etheric realms. As a stone of tranquillity and contentment, it can also dispel anger, irritability, mood swings, fear and negativity. Amethyst can act as a compassionate anchor and ensures that you are emanating your energy from a place of peace and understanding. Wear or use some of this beautiful purple-hued stone to elevate you to higher places today! After all, your dreams are waiting for you to join them up there … it's high time to heed their call.

AQUARIAN POWER CRYSTALS

Around six thousand years ago, in ancient Mesopotamia, the Sumerians started studying precious stones and minerals, as well as the stars, with a view of improving their lives in many ways by probing the secrets and mysteries of the Universe. Their esoteric interests and knowledge were such that they began to grasp the general connections between the Earth and the heavens, or the solar system as they knew it, and the functions of stones and minerals as a link between the two. Their method of making these connections was by colour (for example the Sun was allocated all yellow stones), as well as other spiritual links. The gemstones listed for the portion of your zodiac sign are given their status as your 'power crystals' due to the links that can be made between your primary planetary ruler and your mutable planetary ruler (listed last), and each stone's particular colour, chemical and mineral compositions, healing properties, and the number they are given (based on the Mohs scale of hardness: for example, diamond scores a perfect 10 out of 10), all of which combine to align with your planetary rulers. Working mindfully with your planet's special crystals is one way you can increase the flow of power and magic into your life.

POWER CRYSTALS FOR FIRST HALF AQUARIANS ★ (20 January - 3 February)

Influenced by Uranus, Saturn and Mercury

Peridot, Brazilianite, Aventurine, Onyx, Wulfenite

PERIDOT ★ This crystal belongs to the olivine family and displays a charming range of greens, from pale to dramatic. The deep olive coloured Peridot, which has yellow lights radiating from its depths and is completely transparent, albeit sometimes with a slightly cloudy surface, is the most appropriate for those born in the second half of Aquarius. The Pharaohs of ancient Egypt considered Peridot to be the property of their gods, and it was traditionally used to keep evil spirits away. It is still considered, and used as, a protective stone and is beneficial to the aura. A power cleanser and tonic, it releases and neutralises toxins on all levels and purifies the mind and body. It opens, cleanses and activates the Heart and Solar Plexus chakras and clears burdens, bitterness, greed, guilt, obsessions, unhelpful thoughts and 'baggage'. Peridot assists you to move forward, detach yourself from outside influences, and encourages you to look to your own higher energies for spiritual guidance. An effective mind-sharpener, it aids in learning how to forgive yourself and to step forth and take responsibility for your own life. It enhances confidence and assertion, and alleviates resentment, jealousy, anger, spite and hurts from the past. A generally revitalising and energising stone, it can help to banish lethargy, apathy and exhaustion. Mentally, it motivates growth and enhances transformation through making necessary changes in your life and promotes overall psychological wellbeing, clarity and ultimately, spiritual truth. Peridot is a visionary crystal, which helps you to discover your destiny and your spiritual purpose, making it an excellent working stone for healers - and of course for the naturally far-sighted Aquarian spirit.

BRAZILIANITE ★ As its names suggests, this precious stone is found in Brazil (and the USA) and is an attractive bright yellow to yellowish-green gem. Brazilianite, resonating with the Solar Plexus and Sacral chakras, embodies a potent energy and profound vibration, enhancing creative abilities and guiding our journeys into past lives. This golden stone can cleanse your current life's past and re-empower you spiritually. Its stimulation of the Solar Plexus chakra can help aid manifestation and its loving heart-based energy can help increase your personal power, especially if used with focused intention and integrity. Its hardness (5 out of 10) and colour align it with Mercury's energy.

AVENTURINE ★ Coming in hues of green, blue, yellow, red, pink and glowing sunset, Aventurine is a unique member of the quartz family and owes it fine gold-speckled appearance to tiny flakes of Mica in its body. Green Aventurine is considered the 'opportunity, chance and luck stone'. Connected with the Heart chakra, it helps us to recognise opportunities and is said to place us exactly where we need to be for good things to transpire, as energetically it opens our mind to increased perception and creative insights, so that we are better able to recognise favourable circumstances. Aventurine encourages leadership, decisiveness, compassion, empathy, creativity and perseverance, and defuses negative situations and emotions. It also promotes new growth, optimism, and is an attractor of luck, wealth and prosperity. Aventurine is a stone of comfort and balance, encourages regeneration, opens the heart and restores trust, so is an excellent stone for those who find it difficult to open up their hearts to giving and receiving love. Overall, it stimulates wellbeing, joy and calm, and enables you to live within your own centre.

POWER CYSTALS FOR SECOND HALF AQUARIANS ★ (4 - 18 February)

Influenced by Uranus, Saturn and Venus

Star Diopside, Tugtupite, Jade, Casiterite, Charoite, Torbetine

STAR DIOPSIDE ★ The resplendent Star Diopside can display a four-rayed hovering star with two sharp and two muted lines, hanging suspended over an almost opaque black-green to brownish-black body. Possibly the only top grade magnetic gemstone,

Star Diopside contains needle-like crystals of magnetite that add to its beauty. It has a hardness of 5.5, placing it in the vicinity of Venus's 6. Its beauty aligns it with Venus's vibrations, its colour with Saturn, and its surprising and unusual appearance with Uranus.

JADE ★ Jade belongs to the Nephrite family. It is a serenity stone and is excellent for healing conditions associated with stress and feelings of overwhelming obligation. A wonderful ally in healing others, Jade is a good stone for those who are beginner healers or who wish to give their healing skills an added boost. The ancients considered Jade a sacred stone and it was traditionally worn as a stone of good fortune. On a spiritual level Jade has an affinity for the Heart chakra and it harmonises relationships, encourages compassion and the establishment of strong bonds, and balances the nervous system, dispelling moods swings and calming anger and irritability. It brings serenity when it is worn, carried or used, and instils wisdom, promotes feelings of tranquillity, cleanses feelings and stabilises the personality. Jade is also a useful 'dream' stone; placed under your pillow, it will help you to not only remember your dreams, but also to interpret them. In addition, as a stone of wisdom, it assists us to reach decisions about meaningful things.

CHAROITE ★ This is an expensive stone that is only found in one location in Russia, and its rarity makes it hard to come by. Its colours include pink, lilac, lavender, violet and purple. Having a particular affinity for the Brow, Crown and Heart chakras, it allows us to connect with the spiritual dimensions while still remaining grounded. Charoite is a stone of transformation, a soulful gem which stimulates inner vision, spiritual wisdom and vibrational change. It encourages a path of service to humanity, making it an ideal stone for the global-minded Aquarian. Charoite also alleviates deep fears, compulsions, obsessions and frustrations, and enhances drive, vigour, perspective, acceptance of others and unconditional love. Furthermore, it encourages deep, peaceful sleep and bestows powerful dreams, while at the same time warding off nightmares. It has the ability to transform fear into insight and eases emotional turmoil. This stone, if you can find one, is a magical and mysterious dream-fulfiller with the ability to transform and manifest our deepest desires. A stone of prophecy, Charoite assists us in understanding our visions. Violet-coloured crystals such as Charoite will help take you into a fantasy world, in which you can create or alter your reality. They can open the doors to other realms, release our fears, and remove obstacles from our paths. Charoite is ultimately a cleanser and transmuter of negativity, clearing the aura and chakras, enabling us to express our unconditional love by opening up our hearts and spirits.

YOUR LUCKY NUMBERS

Your lucky numbers are: 2 for Aquarius, 4 for Uranus, 7, and 8 for Saturn (your traditional ruler).

YOUR LUCKY DAY & LUCKY 'MAGIC HOURS' OR 'TIME UNITS'

One rule of magic, luck and power, as already outlined elsewhere in this book, can be found within the well-known phrase, "As above, so below." From the most ancient times, the planets were said to rule earthly destinies and powers. Days of the week were named after the seven planets which were the only ones then known: Sun Day, Moon Day, Mars Day (French: Mardi), Mercury Day (French: Mercredi), Jove Day (French: Jeudi), Venus Day (French: Vendredi) and Saturn Day.

The planetary hours are based on an ancient astrological system, the Chaldean order of the planets. The Chaldean order indicates the relative orbital velocity of the planets, and from a heliocentric (helios = The Sun) perspective, this sequence also indicates the relative distance of the planets from the Sun (the Sun switching places with the Earth in this sequence), and the distance of the Moon from the Earth.

The planetary hours system uses this Chaldean order to divide time, and each planetary hour of the planetary day is ruled by a different planet. The order is repeated, starting with the slowest: Saturn - then, Jupiter, Mars, Sun, Venus, Mercury, Moon, then back to Saturn, Jupiter, Mars, etc, ad infinitum. The planet that rules the first hour of the day is also the ruler of that whole day and gives the day its name. So the first hour of Saturday is ruled by Saturn, the first hour of Sunday by the Sun, and so on. It is important, for the purposes of using specific planetary energies for our magic and wishes, to note that planetary hours are not considered the same length as our normal time-keeping slots of sixty minutes. Each day is split into time periods, daytime and night time, beginning at around sunrise and sunset respectively. These two time periods are each divided into twelve equal-length hours, which are the planetary hours. So the planetary hours of the day and the planetary hours of the night will be of different lengths, except during the equinoxes when light and darkness are balanced.

In sequence, the Sun, Moon and the five visible planets each exerts its own special influence over a twenty four hour period. I like to call your planet's special day and hour the 'Magic Hour'.

Magic rituals to draw luck and love to you should be conducted at astrologically correct times and with the appropriate instruments, tools, cards, herbs, flowers, oils and plants which are linked with the ruling planet. For example a love ritual, spell or potion demands a concoction of any or all of the above ruled by Venus. Do not be ignorant to rulerships, for they wield an unseen power that can help make our dreams, big and small, come true.

Further, as specific hours of each day are ruled by certain planets, if you are really serious about attracting some power, luck or magic into your life, it is imperative that you wish, pray or ask at the most opportune times for your Sun sign. There are two methods you can use for finetuning your magical workings. The first method is to perform your spell, ritual or wishing on the day your Sun sign's ruling planet during the planetary hour that signifies the essence of what you are asking for (e.g. An Aquarius who is looking for love might perform a love-seeking ritual on a Saturday, during a Venus-ruled planetary hour). Alternatively, if you wish to summon the power of your Sun sign's own ruling planet, then that same Aquarian might perform their love-seeking ritual on a Friday (ruled by Venus) during Saturn's planetary hour.

The nature of that which you are asking for, such as love, travel opportunities, money, career guidance, protection or friendship for example, should always be considered when choosing the day or hour during which your magic will be heightened.

The answer to the question why are there seven days in a week, is a very important one to know in unravelling the secret of your Magic Hours. Ancient people recognised the supreme importance of the seven heavenly spheres, which comprised those which could be seen by the naked eye: the Sun, Moon, Mercury, Venus, Mars, Jupiter and Saturn. They then named each of the seven days of the week after one of those spheres and assigned that planetary 'ruler' to one day of the week. As viewed from Earth, these seven spheres appear to move at varying speeds, and the ancients used this factor to arrange them in order of varying speed. If you intend to use your Magic Hours to attract wonderful things, you must memorise that sequence because it is what forms the basis of the whole system.

Whenever you intend to use your Magic Hours, it is important to find out the exact time of sunrise for the area in which you live, as sunrise marks the time when your planet's magic is at its most powerful on its specific day. So, at sunrise on Sunday, the Sun rules the hour following the sunrise, the Moon rules the first hour following sunrise on a Monday, and through the week the pattern is repeated, with each day's ruling planet beginning the cycle in that first hour after dawn. It is logical then, that the rest of the planets, in sequence, follow on with one planet per hour for that day thereafter for the rest of the 24 hour cycle, creating a Magic Hour for each planet throughout the day and night, depending on which planet rules that particular day and is therefore the first in line.

Although this wonderful method of using astrology is very ancient, it may be completely new to you. You are in for a pleasant surprise though, because if you are willing to put the system to the test, rich rewards are in store for you.

YOUR LUCKY DAY: SATURDAY

Saturday is the day of Saturn, your traditional (or secondary) ruler. In the folk rhyme 'Monday's Child', 'Saturday's child works hard for a living'. It is a day of Leadership, Ambition, Authority, Hard Work, Perseverance, Dedication, Responsibility and Duty, and an opportune day for making wishes or working magic involving long-term goals, careers, institutions, establishments, security, investments, karma, 'reversals', building structure, protection, solitude, privacy, determination, endings, blocking, renewing and transforming. Although these words are more aligned with Capricorn, as your modern ruler Uranus does not have rulership over any day of the week, Aquarians can still make good use of these activities and qualities given Saturn's co-rulership over their sign.

SATURN'S MAGIC TIME UNITS (BASED ON THE PLANETARY HOURS) FOR EACH DAY OF THE WEEK

SATURDAY ★ First and Eighth hour after sunrise

SUNDAY ★ Fifth and Twelfth hour after sunrise

MONDAY ★ Second and Ninth Hour after sunrise

TUESDAY ★ Sixth hour after sunrise

WEDNESDAY ★ Third and Tenth hour after sunrise

THURSDAY ★ Seventh hour after sunrise

FRIDAY ★ Fourth and Eleventh hour after sunrise
**

** Please note that for the purposes of simplification, the above information regarding 'Saturn's Magic Time Units' is a very diluted and simplified version of using magical times to your advantage. These hours cover only daylight hours, or the first twelve hours after sunrise, and do not take into account magical times after sunset or throughout the night. 'Hours' is also a deceptive term, as most 'time periods' used in this system are less than an hour, but for the purposes of simplifying the technique, I refer to them as Magic Hours (to keep with the tradition of the term 'planetary hours') rather than magic 'time units', which is what they really are. Should you wish to do further research on your ruling planet's most powerful time units, or require further information about the planet/s from which you are seeking 'energy' from in order to assist your wish-making, other sources may provide you with more comprehensive and detailed information.

YOUR LUCKY CHARM/TALISMANS

The following are three 'materials' or talismanic symbols from which to make your lucky charms, and the planetary energy under which to do it, corresponding with your Sun sign:

AQUARIUS ★ Amethyst, Key, Lead, Saturn

You can also use general charms, such as a cross or a universally lucky symbol, but you will exude and therefore attract more power and protection if you make and wear the appropriate charms with the matching gemstone, set in the right metal and created under the corresponding planetary influence. While most people wear silver or gold, cheaper tin or lead may be more appropriate and beneficial for your Sun sign. An amulet (for protection) or a talisman or charm (for luck), must also be made, ordered, designed or purchased on the appropriate day of the week for its power to be most effective. Your day, as previously described, is Saturday.

You can even go further and create or buy your amulet or charm at one of the hours and/or days when your planet is exerting its most powerful influence. It may sound complicated and requiring of forethought and effort, but if you are going to summon magic and are superstitious enough to truly *believe* that you can do this (and remember pure belief in something is the starting point of manifestation), you should be scrupulous enough to do it properly. For your planet's day and time, please consult the information under the previous headings 'Your Lucky Day' and 'Saturn's Magic Time Units'.

GODS, GODDESSES, ANIMAL TOTEMS & OTHER 'GUIDES'

Gods, goddesses and guides can be summoned to help you live your life to its optimal best. Some are connected with your Sun sign, while others may be of your own personal choosing, ones you may feel particularly drawn towards. Those which align with your ruling planet and your Sun sign, give a good indication of those who will shine a guiding light along your desired path, but you can choose your own too, based upon exploration, observations, research, meditation or simple intuition - I believe choosing your own, based on your inner *knowing* or guidance system, is a very powerful magical tool. However, to get you started, I have listed some below for your contemplation. Good luck!

YOUR LUCKY ANIMALS & BIRDS

Dog, Vulture, Cuckoo, Peacock, Albatross, Phoenix,
Large Birds Which Fly Afar, Otter

Some astrological systems, such as Shamanistic or Native American Astrology, tell us that the Sun sign we were born under has a corresponding animal totem, which tells us about our characteristics and act as a kind of spiritual guide or mentor throughout our life's journey. These totems are described as Solar totems, because many of them share similarities with the solar system and the sign the Sun was passing through at the time of our birth, and therefore relate to animals and animal behaviours which also correspond to environmental conditions and seasonal changes. These animals encompass many aspects of the solar system, from seasonal relationships, to creature instincts, to reciprocal links with the planetary vibrations, and 'clans' within nature that you are inherently closely connected with through your date of birth.

Your Solar totem animal is not the same as an animal spirit guide, which is based on metaphysical principles and is also based on your soul's mission in this embodiment - however, you can definitely make your birth Solar totem animal your spiritual guide if you wish, as you may find that its qualities, traits, symbolism and messages strongly reflect and define your own nature - or what you aspire to become, manifest or draw towards you. Your birth totem power animal comes from a place of trust and innocence, and represents the essence of your creative inner child. If you spend some time meditating on your Solar totem animal, asking what lessons it can teach, and reflect deeply on its character, life and habits, you may find it connects with you on a deep spiritual level and you can make the necessary changes to your life to draw in more magic and power.

YOUR FEATURE ANIMAL ★ OTTER

The Otter's Message ★ The application of spiritual knowledge, play, fun and wisdom to daily earthly life. If you go with the natural ebbs and flows of life, you will discover joy, wonder and simple pleasures

Brings the totem gift of ★ Perception, inventiveness, playfulness and original thinking

Shares the power energies of ★ Tolerance, courage, originality, invention and exuberance

Brings forth and teaches the magic of ★ Creativity, the attaining of wisdom, the acquisition of knowledge, and the value of play, imagination, spontaneity and joy

Being a water creature, the otter's symbolism is linked to the divine and primal feminine, its watery habitat symbolising water as the giver and elixir of life. As the Solar totem and spirit animal guide for the Water Bearer, the otter can remind Aquarians of the importance of play, good-natured rough handling, frolicking, laughter, pure joy and spontaneous, spirited romps with others. Having few enemies in the wild, the otter can also impart lessons in feelings of wellbeing, security and fearlessness. Joyful, agile and nimble, the otter represents agility, curiosity, energy, dexterity, creativity and playfulness. Further, otters are commonly regarded as lucky animals. They feature as light-hearted tricksters in most folklore, and although their exploits are mischievous, they are generally not considered malicious or aggressive.

If you are feeling a little depleted in energy or enjoyment, try calling upon the otter to enliven your soul and restore your spirit. It might even stir you to dance with life and will almost definitely loosen you up and help to re-program the value of play. The more serious side of the otter is that they can be a little quirky and unorthodox, making the otter sometimes difficult to figure out. Although unconventional and misunderstood, the otter's methods are usually very effective. The otter may have an odd way of doing, expressing or perceiving things, but is blessed with a brilliant imagination and intelligence, giving him/her an edge over all others. Perceptive, friendly, intuitive, dynamic, sharing and attentive, the otter may be rebellious at times, but is also truthful, loyal, sympathetic and courageous. Through the otter we learn the courage to open up through play, to surrender to the trust that our needs will always be met, and to experience the bliss of pure and simple pleasures.

SPIRITUAL KEEPER ★ BUFFALO

Your spiritual keeper guides your spiritual growth and brings illumination. The Buffalo (or Bison) is a revered symbol and a mighty albeit confronting animal, each beast weighing up to a tonne. It teaches us the gifts of provision, gratitude, abundance, prosperity, blessing, stability, consistency and strength. Its medicine includes manifestation, protection, earth creativity, courage, knowledge, generosity, sharing, and giving for the greater good. The Buffalo brings you the endurance and power to walk the Great Road of pure intent that leads to happiness, health and fulfilment, bringing the sustenance that offers renewal and rebirth after a long, arduous winter. The Buffalo is a reminder of the greater whole and its symbolism illustrates, in magical ways, the interconnectedness of everything in the world - and the wider Universe. Your animal keeper the Buffalo is, above all, a potent symbol of oneness and abundance.

CLAN ★ BUTTERFLY

Your clan animal comes from a place of inner knowing and intuition, helping you to discover the essence and magic of your true self. The Butterfly, a Totem of the Air clan, represents and protects all that is beautiful and holds the secrets of change and personal transformation. The Butterfly symbolises that this transformation is always available to you, and may even begin without your conscious participation. It symbolises metamorphosis, teaches us to trust in the process of change, re-awakens us to joy, and teaches us that life is full of surprises and to therefore live with a constant sense of passion, intensity and wonder.

YOUR METALS

Aquarian power metals are uranium, platinum, lead and aluminium.

URANIUM

Uranium is a very heavy metal which contains an abundant source of concentrated energy. Discovered in the eighteenth century, it is the principal fuel for nuclear reactors and the main raw material for nuclear weapons. It is no coincidence that the element associated with atomic energy is uranium, for the enormous power of the atom is equal to the power of Uranus. There are two ways to release this atomic power: through fission and through fusion. In fission, the heaviest atoms are split apart, and the resulting release of energy deposits radioactive waste which is extremely difficult to deal with, and potentially lethal to all life on our planet. In fusion, however, the lightest atoms are fused together, and the resulting release of energy does not pose a risk by leaving radioactive waste. Therefore, it makes sense that we can use this latter process to benefit mankind without the ominous possibility of destroying that which we are trying to improve. Uranus usually has the best of intentions, especially when it comes to serving humanity, so utilising it for the benefit of all, rather than the potential destruction of all, is undoubtedly far more desirable.

PLANTS, HERBS, SPICES, TREES, SHRUBS, FLOWERS, SCENTS & INCENCE

Different scents, herbs, flowers and plants have their own specific vibrations. Their essences should be worn on your skin (you can make up your own combinations using essential oils or flower waters), burned in an oil burner, inhaled from a cloth, diffused in a bath or bowl of steam, or burned as incense sticks. Many plants, herbs and spices, however used, contain gentle yet effective energies which will affect not only your wishing ceremonies, but also your moods, associations and emotions, which can assist in carrying your wonderful self in the direction of your dreams. Lifted up on incense smoke, for example, your 'wish' is carried out to the wider Universe. Try making your own, out of any or all of your power plants, woods, flowers, shrubs, trees or herbs!

YOUR LUCKY PLANTS, HERBS, SPICES, TREES, SHRUBS, FLOWERS, SCENTS, OILS & INCENSE

Pine, cypress, frankincense, passionflower, barley, snake root, skullcap, marshmallow, prickly ash, valerian, lady's slipper, hops, myrrh, rowan, apple blossom, orchid, pear, dancing lady, mandrake, golden-rain, snowdrop, chamomile, catnip, southernwood, elder, fuchsia, foxglove, mountain ash, most fruit trees. *

YOUR FOODS

Aquarians love to experiment with new ideas, methods, foods, dishes and recipes - if indeed they follow recipes at all; most will invent their own concoctions as they go. If you're a truly typical Aquarian you'll adore eating out, and the more varied, eclectic and obscure the cuisine the better. You often enjoy the discovery of new tastes and textures more than the actual act of eating them. The person who samples Cambodian fried tarantulas, Vietnamese snake wine, Australian witchetty grubs, Indonesian luwak excrement, is likely to be born under the sign of Aquarius; the quirkier the dish, the more appealing it will be! Furthermore, you love to eat meals or unusual foods that can provide a fascinating conversation-starter for the next dinner party. Boring, bland or tedious is definitely not on the menu for the Water Bearer.

Your power foods are health foods, peppers, limes, star fruit, chillies, kiwi fruits, dried fruits, kumquats, and foods with sharp, distinctive or unusual flavours.
*

* Caution: Always use essential oils and/or herbs with caution and research each one prior to use, as

not all are safe for use by certain people, or under certain conditions such as pregnancy, intoxication or illness. Some herbs and oils may be hallucinogenic, toxic in high doses, or produce other undesirable effects, and may be considered potentially harmful or hazardous if used or consumed before operating machinery, driving, or combined with alcohol or other drugs. Always consult a qualified practitioner or undertake thorough research from reliable sources before use or consumption of any of the above essential oils, herbs or foods.

YOUR LUCKY WOOD

PINE (Great to make a magic wand out of!)

Pine wood corresponds to the elements of Fire and Air, and is purifying and cleansing to your physical environment, your personal 'space' and your overall person. It is excellent for attracting prosperity and to keep you 'on course' when your life or dreams seem to have deviated off their intended paths; its grace and stateliness serves as a reminder to always look upwards and to think positively. It also brings about inner peace, serenity, tranquillity, fertility, abundance, health, love and optimism. Excellent for use in rising above difficulties, pine is ultimately cleansing, uplifting, rejuvenating, purifying, and sanctifying. Pine cones, branches and needles also contain unique magical powers. Pine needles and boughs are especially good for bringing luck and prosperity, while pine cones are a potent symbol of fertility. Hanging pine in any form above the doorway or mantel of your house is believed to bring good fortune to those who dwell therein.

THE POWER OF LOVE

Each Sun sign exudes their own love and romance style. This style is an energy unique to that sign, and has the power to magnetise to that person their true, soulful match. Unhappy or unsuccessful relationships are often the result of incompatible Sun signs, personal values, goals, hopes, viewpoints or expectations. I believe everyone has a perfect soul partner (or three!) who is especially for them, and just knowing that special person or persons are out there can illuminate your life's romantic path. In this lifetime, we may not find that person or persons, but can still experience the joys and wonders of many other significant relationships which enrich and add tremendous meaning to our lives. Some partnerships are only fleeting, but the feelings they give us can last a lifetime, while others are more enduring, and the rewards they give us and lessons they teach us can last a lifetime too. Small gestures of love on a frequent basis, consistent nurturing and communication, and making the effort to understand each other, are just four ways to keep the fires of passion and romance burning long after the initially roaring fire has diminished into glowing embers.

Your whole natal chart would need to be looked at to form an overall picture of your romantic nature, and although the Sun is a fantastic starting point, it is not the sole consideration. Regarding these other planets, in Carl Jung's studies on psychological astrology, and in traditional synastry (the comparing of two people's natal charts to determine overall compatibility), the harmonious link between the Sun in one person's chart and the Moon in the other's (usually the man's Sun and the woman's Moon) is considered the best indication for a happy and enduring relationship. More specifically, the sextile aspect, an angle of 60 degrees, appeared most frequently between the Sun of one and the Moon of the other. Other positive planetary contacts, such as one person's Moon to another's Venus, or the Mars to the Moon (again, traditional indications of attraction and harmony) also occurred frequently.

The feminine personal planets in a male's chart (Moon and Venus), and the masculine personal planets in a female's chart (Sun and Mars) tell a lot about the inner self and how this is projected onto relationships. However helpful chart analysis is in telling a story about your relationship style and approach, it all depends not on your chart, but on what you do with the resources at your disposal, which your chart can tell you a lot about. Relationships and marriages involving harmonious planetary and zodiacal energies between the two people tend to last longer because they are simply more 'flowing' and easier.

The signs in which the four personal and 'relationship' planets - the Sun, the Moon, Venus and Mars - are placed, coupled with the aspects they make with the other planets in the chart, give important clues into understanding the often unconscious drives within you that shape your relationship style, mannerisms and patterns.

Expanding upon the other planetary considerations is beyond the scope of this book, but it is useful to know, particularly if you are interested in examining the dynamics of a current relationship a bit deeper, or are wishing to attract a new one into your life. But for now, your Sun sign is a wonderful place to start! Your solar sign is regarded as being at the core of the complex - and very fun - study of relationships! So for now, we will begin this study of love with your essence, your core self, the brightest light shining from within - your Sun sign!

SOME LOVE TIPS

★ GEMSTONES ★

The general rule is that any of the pink or green stones are closely aligned with matters of the heart and will help you to entice the affections you seek. Although your Sun sign has its very own special gemstones, outlined elsewhere in the book, the following crystals can be used by all the signs (except for the first point, which are your own sign's feature stones), as their energies and qualities contain the power to attract and create love in all its forms, from self-love to deeper soulful connections with another, or to increase states of being which enhance your abilities to magnetise love.

★ Amethyst, garnet and aquamarine: Using your Aquarius's luckiest crystals are a fabulous start to working on heightening your romantic zest, and making your sensual energy more potent. Zircon, jacinth and jargoon are also useful in raising your attracting powers.

★ Rose quartz is the ultimate love stone. It invites love into your life by helping to open your heart to receive love, and gently reminding you that you are worthy of love. Connected with the heart chakra, it is the stone of unconditional love, enhancing all forms of love and opening up the heart. It is excellent for increasing self-worth and acceptance. Balancing and calming, it helps to heal emotional pain. Wear this stone or keep some beside your bed, or sleep with some under your pillow to remind you that love it coming your way.

★ Green Aventurine is considered the 'opportunity and luck stone'. Connected with the heart chakra, it helps us to recognise opportunities and is set to place us exactly where we need to be for good things to transpire, as energetically it opens our mind and heart to increased perception to recognise lucky elements. It also promotes new growth, optimism, and is an attractor of luck, love and abundance. Aventurine is a stone of comfort and balance, encourages regeneration, opens the heart and restores trust, so is an excellent stone for those who find it difficult to open up their hearts to love.

★ Malachite helps to usher away hurtful memories and works quickly and diligently to clear away painful heartache to make way for new connections. This is a stone of alignment and is excellent to use in self-exploration journeys. It is regarded as "the mirror of the soul" and so some crystal experts may warn against wearing malachite as it may prove too powerful and confronting for some. Wear this stone over your heart chakra, or sleep with it under your pillow.

★ Jade, on a spiritual level, has an affinity with the heart chakra. It harmonises relationships, and encourages compassion and the establishment of strong bonds.

★ Rhodochrosite can be used to attract one's soul mate. This stone, as with all the pink stones, can be used as an effective love magnet. It encourages you to appreciate yourself by teaching you that you are worthy of love, wholeness and happiness - and so opening you up to receive.

★ Rhodonite embodies heart-based energy and stimulate acceptance and forgiveness. Rhodonite is a great stone of forgiveness, helping you to forgive yourself and others, in order to create some new, energised space in which to receive love.

★ Citrine instils courage, self-confidence and joy. It will help to make you feel more empowered, confident and self-assured. Connected with the solar plexus chakra, this stone carries the power of the Sun. It is associated with good fortune, luck, abundance, manifestation, and increases personal power and energy. Highly solar in nature, citrine promotes clarity and puts us in touch with celestial fire and the powers of our brightest luminary and the core essence of our self, the Sun. It can enliven you and connect you strongly with the light of your inner being. Carry this stone or wear it as jewellery to make you feel more sunny, courageous, joyful, bold - and more open to receiving.

★ Moonstone opens the mind to hoping and wishing, inspiration and impulse, synchronicity and serendipity. It grants intuitive recognition and even flashes of insight, and allows one to absorb what is needed from the Universe.

★ Beryl, emerald, ruby, garnet and lapis lazuli are also known for their love properties, and can be used to invite romance into your life, and worn or used to bring or retain love.

★ ESSENTIAL OILS ★

The following essential oils are known for their aphrodisiac or love-attracting properties also, and can be worn as perfumes on the skin, used in an oil burner or vapouriser, used in spell-casting and wishing rituals, sprinkled on your pillow to imbue your dreams with inspired romantic notions or in any other creative ways you can think of! **

★ Rose is traditionally accepted as the fragrance of love, blessed with a reputation for opening up the hearts of all those who come under its spell.

★ Generally any essential oil which promotes relaxation helps open us up to love. These include, but are not limited to: Neroli, geranium, lavender and ylang ylang.

★ Sandalwood, patchouli, vetiver, vanilla, rose otto, orange, cedarwood, ginger, bergamot, rosewood, clary sage, and jasmine are also exquisitely seductive and sensual, and can be used in any way you like to bring to you that which your heart desires.

** Always research first and use with caution.

AQUARIUS ★ LOVE STYLE

To Aquarius love is open and friendly, but you may come across glamorously aloof. As a lover and in relationships, you are afraid of deep emotional involvement and may find it difficult to sustain close relationships, because this means adjusting your lifestyle to accommodate the habits of another, but are extremely loyal and faithful once committed. You value friendship above all else, and in any close relationship you tend to guard your independence and freedom, and often enjoy unconventional or even living-apart relationships. You like your partner to share or even take over the chores of the home, as housework hinders your much-valued liberty. You expect your partner to allow you personal freedom of movement and action, have a respect for your many friends, and have an understanding and tolerance of your oddities, and in return you offer unwavering loyalty and faithfulness. If your relationship is based on friendship, it is more likely to endure than one that isn't. For you after all, lust, passion and sex need a solid base.

AQUARIUS ★ COMPATIBILITY

* Please note the following is based on Sun signs alone. For a whole and integrated approach to relationship compatibility, your whole natal chart would need to be taken into consideration. For the purposes of length, the below information is simplified and only refers to Sun sign connections.

Aquarius ★ Aries

The interaction between the ruling planets of these two, Mars and Uranus, and their respective elements, Air and Fire, ensures there will indeed be tremendous power between these two. Aquarius will never hamper Aries' independence or initiative, and Aries is likely to feel inspired by Aquarius' lively and friendly company. Aries loves anything novel, so Aquarius' offbeat character will appeal, but the hot-headed and passionate Ram is likely to become impatient and irritated with the Water Bearer's unpredictability, cool indifference and aloofness at times. Aries will also not always readily tolerate the 'embrace-all-peace-love-and-brotherhood' attitude of Aquarius, as Aries likes to always be right in the centre of the (relationship's) Universe. If used constructively, however, this is a wonderful match which will fulfil, uplift and inspire both signs. *Overall compatibility rating: 8 out of 10.*

Lucky Power Tip: To attract an Aries, wear the colours red or orange, and wear the crystal diamond.

Aquarius ★ Taurus

Very different in nature, these two have little in common but their more negative expressions, such as stubbornness, unwillingness to change and inflexibility. Taurus is possessive while Aquarius values freedom; Taurus is affectionate while Aquarius is generally undemonstrative; Taurus is simple while Aquarius embraces complexities; Taurus is sensual and seeks security while Aquarius is experimental and seeks novel experiences; Taurus is traditional while Aquarius challenges the establishment; Taurus is domestic while Aquarius loathes being chained to the kitchen sink; Taurus deals with tangible and practical realities while Aquarius is idealistic and deals with the abstract and unusual. Both share the Fixed mode, meaning there is a certain obstinacy and potential for frequent locking of horns that may hinder their progress. Taurus finds it difficult to understand Aquarius's unconventional and unpredictable nature, while Aquarians spread themselves far and wide socially, finding it difficult to fulfil Taurus's need for exclusivity in a relationship. *Overall compatibility rating: 5 out of 10.*

Lucky Power Tip: To attract a Taurus, wear the colours pink or green, and wear the crystal rose quartz.

Aquarius ★ Gemini

Both thinking and mentally-oriented Air signs, these two have the potential to make beautiful music together. Gemini can usually accept Aquarius's erratic and detached moods, and both will give each other the space they need in the relationship. Gemini is stimulated by Aquarius's dazzling intellect and Aquarius in turn is inspired by Gemini's lively mind. The Fixed, headstrong, stubborn characteristics of the Water Bearer may be trying for the Twins' fickle, Mutable, flexible nature, and Gemini's restlessness may make Aquarius dizzy at times. These two can usually work through most differences, however, and there will never be a dull moment, especially in the social arena, in which they both spend most of their time. The unconventional and changeable quality of this relationship helps to keep it interesting, and neither is likely to smother the other, but these two may be so busy mingling in their many separate activities and friendship circles that they forget to make time for each other! *Overall compatibility rating: 9 out of 10.*

Lucky Power Tip: To attract a Gemini, wear the colours light blue or yellow, and wear the crystal citrine.

Aquarius ★ Cancer

The ruling planets of these two, Uranus and the Moon respectively, exercise two very different energies in the relationship. Further, their two respective elements, Air and Water, and their modes, Fixed and Cardinal, don't blend easily. The Crab will prove too emotional and clingy for the intellectually-inclined, freedom-seeking Aquarius, and Cancer will find Aquarius's naturally cool and aloof nature unsettling, and perhaps even hurtful to their highly sensitive nature. Cancer is private while Aquarius loves to share; Cancer is personal while Aquarius is impersonal; Cancer is home-loving while Aquarius feels stifled when domestically 'caged in'; Cancer seeks sentimental love and a meeting of the hearts, while Aquarius seeks friendship and a meeting of the minds. Overall, Aquarius is a universal rather than a personal lover, who likes to share interests and ideas with friends and humanity, and Cancer has a protective, security-seeking nature whose interests lie primarily in their homes, children and families. *Overall compatibility rating: 5 out of 10.*

Lucky Power Tip: To attract a Cancerian, wear the colours silver or white, and wear the crystal moonstone.

Aquarius ★ Leo

While these two are astrological opposites, they are not necessarily psychological opposites, as their respective elements, Air and Fire, blend well together. In fact, being cosmic opposites, they have much to teach each other, and each can learn invaluable relationship lessons from the other. Both being Fixed signs, you also share strong minds, fixed opinions, a strong determination and each a mind of your own. These qualities can be used constructively to form a wonderful bond between you, but there will inevitably be clashes of wills, especially if the Water Bearer takes flight, as they are prone to do from time to time, and the Lion doesn't get his or her way. Leo needs adoration, praise and to be the centre of attention, and will not always appreciate Aquarius's need for sharing and caring on a wider scale. Leo's pride can be easily wounded by Aquarius's independence and lack of consistent affection. Overall, if used positively, Leo and Aquarius can share a joyful and stimulating relationship, if they can overcome their differences. Indeed, Air will usually fuel the Fire here, making it burn bigger and brighter. *Overall compatibility rating: 7 out of 10.*

Lucky Power Tip: To attract a Leo, wear the colours gold or orange, and wear the crystal ruby.

Aquarius ★ Virgo

Air and Earth generally don't blend well together, and although their respective ruling planets, Uranus and Mercury, are similar in nature, this only emphasises a mental and intellectual affinity between these two very different signs, rather than a deep emotional bond. Virgo's nitpicking and fussiness will get on Aquarius's nerves, and Aquarius's unpredictable, temperamental and unconventional nature will unsettle the orderly, rational and sensible Virgo. The Water Bearer's dispassionate, detached and uninvolved character may resonate with the Virgin's naturally cool and essentially unemotional psyche, but Virgo's natural tendency to anxiety and worrying will irk the more broad-minded Aquarius. Virgo can't see the forest for the trees, while the Water Bearer can see the entire forest *and* the trees. Overall, Virgo's need for logic and order are the furtherest things from the erratic Aquarius's mind, and Virgo's natural, almost obsessive, tendencies towards cleanliness and tidiness are not concerns at all for Aquarius. *Overall compatibility rating: 5 out of 10.*

Lucky Power Tip: To attract a Virgo, wear the colours white or yellow, and wear the crystal sapphire.

Aquarius ★ Libra

Air harmonises with Air, and these two have the potential to have an intense and explosive meeting of the minds. Since these two signs are naturally friendly and need the company of others, they can share these pleasures together. However, Libra is the epitome of the personal lover, while Aquarius is the archetypal universal lover who prefers to share interests and affections with many people. Libra's emphasis on close intimate relationships can also cause tension, as Aquarius needs to feel free and unencumbered by emotional ties. While Aquarius is largely aloof, eccentric and unpredictable, Libra uses diplomacy, grace and tact to handle things. Neither will make impossible demands on the other, as both are intellectually-based rather than feeling, smothering types, but this relationship can only work if Libra allows Aquarius freedom and does not demand too much 'together' time. Their intellectual rapport alone, however, suggests deep potential here, and can take their relationship to great heights. *Overall compatibility rating: 8.5 out of 10.*

Lucky Power Tip: To attract a Libran, wear the colours pink and blue, and wear the crystal opal.

Aquarius ★ Scorpio

Air and Water don't tend to blend easily, and this is highlighted in this coupling. Scorpio is intensely emotional and naturally possessive, and this doesn't always sit too well with the freedom-loving, detached and unemotional Aquarius. Scorpio will feel rejected and be left cold by Aquarius's apparent disregard for their complex feelings. If Scorpio tries to dominate the indomitable Aquarius, rebellion will result, and when a serious rift develops in this relationship, Aquarius can easily separate and cut the losses, while Scorpio may brood, sulk and harbour feelings of revenge or vindictiveness. Scorpio is passionate and controlling, while Aquarius is dispassionate and needs space. While the Water Bearer sees love in broader, universal terms, the Scorpion views love in powerfully personal terms. Unless this significant difference in emotions is understood, Scorpio will feel that Aquarius is too indifferent and impersonal. Also, Aquarius's erratic nature will challenge Scorpio's all-or-nothing, extreme attitudes to life. Although there are many differences between you, being Fixed signs, you are both strong-willed and determined, so if you can channel your combined forces into a common goal, great achievements are possible in this relationship. *Overall compatibility rating: 6.5 out of 10.*

Lucky Power Tip: To attract a Scorpio, wear the colours red or burgundy, and wear the crystal malachite.

Aquarius ★ Sagittarius

Air and Fire have a strong affinity, as do the ruling planets of these two, Uranus, the lord of lightning, and Jupiter, the god of thunder. These two will have a wonderful chemistry between them and make a strong impact on each other, but when the need arises, they both give each other the freedom they so desire. Both being independent and intellectual rather than deeply feeling, you share incredibly idealistic natures that usually remain as pie-in-the-sky ideals, but which thrill you nonetheless, and can provide endless fodder for stimulating conversation. Indeed, you both love to share your sparkling ideals which transcend the personal, mundane level. The Archer has an uncanny ability to bring out the passionate side of the Water Bearer, and you are the most likely of all the combinations to be sexually compatible. Sagittarius's warm wit and charm will win over Aquarius's more cool nature, and Aquarius's aloof glamour will appeal to the Sagittarian's accepting and embracing heart. You are both naturally friendly and gregarious, so are likely to attract and enjoy many resulting social pleasures and events together. *Overall compatibility rating: 9 out of 10.*

Lucky Power Tip: To attract a Sagittarius, wear the colour deep purple or royal blue, and wear the crystal zircon.

Aquarius ★ Capricorn

While Aquarius, an Air sign, is erratic, unusual, inventive, unorthodox and more than a little wayward, Capricorn, an Earth sign, is traditional, sensible, practical, conventional and structured. Air and Earth do not mix very harmoniously, and their two respective modes, Fixed and Cardinal, will also prove an obstacle to these two seeing eye to eye. Capricorn is tight, sometimes mean, and tenacious, striving for goals and lofty ambitions, while Aquarius is unpredictable but ever-friendly, and independent, determined to reach their ideals in a completely different way. Aquarian behaviour often undermines Capricorn's desire for stability, security and consistency. The Water Bearer likes to rock the boat, shake up the status quo and seek out thrills, while the Goat is rigid, conservative and respectful. These two share minds of a high order, however, and if they can channel their energies into their intellectual rapport and natural respect for each other, a mutually fulfilling relationship could very well develop. Overall, Aquarius's capriciousness and rebellious streak will unnerve and shock the quiet, steady Goat, who just wants to live a peaceful - albeit constantly achieving - life. *Overall compatibility rating: 6 out of 10.*

Lucky Power Tip: To attract a Capricorn, wear the colours brown or black, and wear the crystal garnet.

Aquarius ★ Aquarius

On the surface, both of you, sharing the same Sun and the same ruling planet, appear to be the picture of excitement, thrills and oddball adventures. However, too much Air may create two people who seem to get along like, well, a hurricane. Outsiders may not be able to fathom this complex Aquarian wavelength because it takes one to know another, and only these two can truly know why the other thinks or behaves as they do. You are both intellectual, independent, freedom-loving and detached, so there is a deep resonance and unspoken understanding at work here. Your ruling planet Uranus, may prove too much of a force and while initially providing fireworks and 'electricity', this energy can just as readily burn you both - or at least give your relationship an unpleasant electric jolt when you least expect it. Much will depend on the many facets of this sign each person reflects, but sooner or later, unusual, surprising or disruptive influences may affect your relationship. It does, however have the potential to be a strong bond, formed through the meeting of two incredibly intuitive, original and brilliant minds - just don't spend too much time apart by working in separate laboratories, or climbing different rainbows.
Overall compatibility rating: 8 out of 10.

Lucky Power Tip: To attract an Aquarian, wear the colours electric blue or turquoise, and wear the crystal aquamarine.

Aquarius ★ Pisces

It would be hard to find a more unusual - and enlightening - combination than these two, for the simple reason that your respective ruling planets, Uranus and Neptune, are quite literally out of this world. Both have an elusive quality about them, and have a level of understanding that seems to contradict the usual Air/Water relating difficulties. You are both unique and different from most other people, and you sometimes feel like misfits, except around each other. Although the Piscean psyche is deep, emotional and complex, the Aquarian can still manage to sense the unfathomable depths in the Piscean soul. Although feeling, sensitive and romantic, the Pisces seems to intuitively respect Aquarius's need for independence, freedom and friendships outside the relationship. These two are both lovers of solitude, for different reasons of course, but they understand each other's occasional need for retreat. If these two can forget their elementary and modal (Fixed and Mutable) differences, they may just make a beautiful symphony together - indeed, they can swim along happily through life's meandering waters together, as long as Pisces doesn't get lost along the way. *Overall compatibility rating: 7.5 out of 10.*

Lucky Power Tip: To attract a Pisces, wear the colours mauve or sea green, and wear the crystal amethyst.

LESSONS TO BE LEARNED FOR GREATER POWER AND LUCK

Aquarian problems and ultimate undoings arise through your contradictory nature, eccentricity, rebelliousness for its own sake, the desire for change to the detriment of all else, and your contradictory and paradoxical tendencies, which often leave others confused, bewildered and unable to rely upon you. Aquarius has two powerful rulers, Saturn being your traditional ruler and Uranus being your modern ruler; both planets exert their own unique influences, and most Aquarians will fall into one category or the other. Saturnian Water Bearers are inclined to be rigid, intense, severe, cool, controlling and may strive to attain their lofty ideals through anarchism. Uranian Water Bearers are unconventional, perverse, contrary and sometimes act up for the mere sake of being different - or difficult! Prone to mental disturbances, this type may also tend towards bouts of anarchy, annihilation, 'stirring the pot', conflicting with authority, shaking up establishments, and all-out rebellion. Indeed, that person who is willing to chain themselves to a tree to confront bulldozers is likely to be a Uranian type, or at the very least have a prominent Aquarius influence in their chart!

The challenge is to learn how to become more cooperative and involve others more in your idealistic goals; you tend to go it alone and usually do so with a stubborn, inflexible manner. If you learn how to reach inside and exude a bit more warmth and concern for others on a personal, individual level, and not just with regard for humanity or groups, you will evolve, grow, glow and simply flow - and maybe even be allowed to keep your rose-coloured glasses on as you go!

YOUR TAROT CARDS - FOR LUCK, MAGIC, ABUNDANCE, ENERGY & MEANING

★ THE STAR ★

Ruled By Aquarius

KEY THEMES

★ A Woman Who is Connected to the Source of Creativity ★ Vision Beyond the Roles We Play in Life to Who We Really Are ★ Rebirth, Renewal ★ Light After Darkness ★ The Calm After the Storm ★ Restored Hope, Faith, Inspiration and Promise ★ A Bright Future ★

Meditation ★ "The energy I pour into today will fuel my whole future."

The Star is a good omen. A fortunate card, it indicates the hope and renewal that occurs after calamity, promising new and rich horizons, perhaps in previously unforeseen directions, but only after you have been tempered and expanded by having come through the storm. It expresses hope, a sense of healing and a return to wholeness, especially after emotional storms, for after the storm, there is peace. This card is the perfect symbol of wholeness, calm, oneness and healing.

It depicts a beautiful naked maiden who pours water from two pitchers; one flows into a pool, representing the depths of the unconscious, and the other onto dry land, representing the conscious mind. She revives the land with the water from the pool, while the morning star heralds the beginning of a new dawn, fresh life and renewed hope. Above her, eight stars (all eight-pointed), symbolising the heavenly or higher realms, shine brightly against the backdrop of a milky night sky on the cusp of daybreak, while a bird perches on a tree in the background and a butterfly flutters overhead. As the maiden reaches out to touch the oneness of all life and all the Universe, the same light that radiates from the stars overhead glows from *her*. The bird sitting in the Tree of Life is the ibis of immortality, a sacred bird, a symbol of the soul's ability to rise to higher levels of emotional and spiritual consciousness. It also represents a symbol of our spiritual self, waiting to drink from the wisdom-bestowing waters of the lake. The butterfly stands for transformation and resurrection.

Like its animal symbols, this card comes after a crisis or 'storm', standing for light coming out of darkness, and offers peace, flow and freedom. In the

Star we see the inner self joyfully experiencing itself. The Star is *free*.

Aquarius, the sign attributed to the Star, is the fixed air sign of the Water Bearer and represents the healing force in the Universe, as well as group understanding, collective sympathies, psychic sensitivities, and universal friendship. Aquarians tend to be visionary in their outlook, and the Star prepares one for initiation, making it an effective symbolic tool for launching oneself off towards a brighter future - one that the Aquarian often envisions in his or her mind and spirit long before anyone else.

A card of enlightenment and enhanced awareness, the Star is symbolic of our faith, our belief in our hopes, and our desire that our wishes will come true, providing a sense of purpose and meaning, without which our lives become dull and lacklustre. It signifies that redemption is possible, that transformative powers are within our reach. It cleanses and releases all pain, restoring happiness and belief. The Star provides that bit of magic that spurs us on, keeping us going during times of stress or doubt. Indeed, the image of the Star reflects the inner light that can guide us through the darkness. The Star is not a card of action, but of inner calm. For the moment, the journey can wait. Destiny will unfold as it will before you.

This card urges you to stay positive, for a goal is at last within your reach. It symbolises insight, understanding and hope for the future, and asks that the spiritual dimension of life should not be ignored.

The idea of wishing upon a star is at the centre of the card's meaning, and it signifies that a wish will come true, something you have hoped for since perhaps you were a child. The wish-granting quality of the Star also shows us that the Universe is not the senseless and unjust place it often appears to be. The Star card suggests that there is always something else, even when the going is really tough. It indicates a gesture of affection, perhaps a gift, but the gifts of the Star are not always material.

Indeed, this card is a good indication that wishes will be fulfilled, not always in the form that one expects, but even so, the unexpected will have a good result. The Star shows good health and that gifts will be given. Some gifts may be in the form of the idea of cosmic power reaching down, blessing our earthly life, bestowing our spirit with joy, and transmitting its healing energy.

Its main divinatory meanings are hope, faith, inspiration, bright prospects, optimism, insight, a mixing of the past and present, spiritual love, astrological influence, fulfilment and pleasure. It signifies the divine balancing of desire and work, love and expression, and hope and effort. It delivers a message of promise, good fortune and joy. It suggests inspiration, a deep sense of purpose, an inner knowing that things will turn out for the best, an intuitive belief in magic, and the renewal of life's force and energy. It promises and encourages imagination and a positive attitude, even when times are difficult or trying.

When the Star card appears in a reading, you know you have passed to a new level and something in you has opened to a higher plane. You are ready to ask for help, and you will receive it. A certain grace comes over you which allows you to see ahead with renewed confidence, and you trust in the ability of the Universe to heal you. You are ready to begin the process of transformation.

This may indicate a time when you have become aware of a divine or higher spirit 'touching' you or drawing you in, and perhaps it is fitting that you choose or are chosen for, a new name for yourself, to signify the newness of your self. Those who have been transformed through the powers of the Star symbolism, have often thereafter adopted a spiritual, ritual or otherwise special name. Listen for yours. It will be unique and have deep symbolic significance for you. Above all, it will represent your reborn, renewed and refreshed self.

An image of belief and promise, the Star indicates a sense of purpose, a goal to reach for and an ambition to aim towards. The sight of the stars at night have long been associated with awe and magic, and the Star appearing in your reading brings with it the hope and assurance that things will come right, even when they have been very difficult. The Star can provide you with a positive outlook and a welcome source of optimism and expectation that will carry you through stormy times.

When working with this card, ask yourself what insights flow from the waters of your unconscious? Now that the Star has lit up your spiritual darkness, it is only a matter of time before you reach the ultimate heights of your journey. The world needs your light and your happiness. Make it a point to shine brightly like the stars this card depicts, and you will reap the benefits from sharing your joy, wisdom and higher self. Ultimately, this card conveys the hopeful message that when we wish upon a star, our dreams come true.

Aquarians are recommended to carry one of these cards with them to illumine their paths, and to magnetise that for which they are asking. Go forth and claim the magic which is yours!

★ THE FOOL ★

Ruled By Uranus and the Element of Air

KEY THEMES

★ Fresh Beginnings ★ Adventure ★ Excitement ★ Spontaneity ★ Egolessness ★ Innocence ★ Naiveté ★ Courage ★ A Happy-Go-Lucky Mortal, About to Step Off a Cliff Into the Abyss ★

Meditation ★ "I have the courage to step forward; I am not afraid of the unknown."

The Fool is usually the first card in the Tarot deck, the starting point of the Tarot 'experience'. In some early decks he appeared at the end of the Major Arcana rather than at the beginning, as he not only begins our journey but may also accompany us throughout it - this is essentially because he symbolises our very self. When he first sets out at the beginning of his path, he is a stranger to his inner self and lives primarily in his conscious mind, but by the end of his journey he has glimpsed the deeper mysteries of his true self. The Fool seeks the truth, and turns his attention towards the spirit in search of it. There is in the Fool an element of the divine trickster, and even though the Fool doesn't know what he is doing in the sense of logical thought, he moves from an impulse that arises out of the infinite possibilities emanating from the state represented by the number 'zero'.

The Fool is simple, innocent, trusting and ignorant of the potential trials, setbacks and pitfalls that await him, and he is prepared to abandon his old ways and follow his quest by taking a leap into the unknown. Indeed, the Fool represents the need to let go of old ways and begin something new, untested and unexperienced. For those willing to follow the Fool's example and deviate from the path society has set out for us, this leap can bring joy, adventure, and finally, for those with the courage to continue even when the path becomes fearsome, the leap will bring peace, knowledge and liberation.

Interestingly, in some early Tarot decks, the Fool appeared as a giant court jester, towering over those around him, his title the 'Fool of God'. The term has also been used for harmless madmen, dim-witted folk and fitful characters, all of whom were thought to be in touch with a greater wisdom only because they were disconnected with the rest of us. This archetype persists in modern mythology (and arguable real life) also.

The card depicts the Fool wandering off, his few possessions slung over his shoulder in a small bag hung from a pilgrim's staff, oblivious to the chasm ahead, with his dog jumping at his leg. His bag carries his experiences. He does not abandon them, for he is not thoughtless, they simply do not control him in the way that our traumas or memories so often control our lives. The stick upon which his bag casually hangs, is actually a wand, a symbol of power and magic. The Fool card's image symbolises the instinctive life force that both holds him back and urges him on. Like its ruler Uranus, the Fool is the spirit of chaos, of the unexpected, but also about innocence and the simple joys of living. This card belongs anywhere in the deck, in combination with and between any of the other cards, offering an animating force to more static images and symbols. He assists during times of transition, and also in times of difficult passage.

Containing all possibilities, the Fool represents the phenomenon of synchronicity or coincidences between happenings, and is the part of us that unconsciousness connects to the greater universal whole, so things are constantly happening to us that involve the unspoken and often unacknowledged links between our thoughts and events outside of ourselves. If you are open to magic, you will accept these synchronicities on an intellectual level, and in turn will notice such events more frequently and learn to embrace and appreciate them more fully.

This card can be said to represent the human soul that is unselfconsciously happy to be alive, that does not yet reflect back upon itself, the spark of life that reincarnates again and again until it truly awakens to itself. Reincarnation is the secret key to the Fool, and the Fool is indeed the 'secret' key, or at least significantly the first door which opens us up to the rest of the Tarot experience. The Fool, whose awareness is limited to the present moment, moves from moment to moment, life to life, without intellectual consideration nor care for what has gone before and what will be in the future. Representing innocence, the Fool is perpetually young and always starting afresh. It believes in itself and automatically trusts its body and the general flow of life.

Astrologically, the Fool is ruled by the Air element, making it as free as the wind. Uranus, considered the most eccentric of the planets, gives the card's symbolism qualities of intellectual brilliance, intuitive flashes, lawlessness, reform, inventiveness and originality. Linked to this rebellious planet, it also promises mystery, a dash of genius, adventure, and a great opportunity to reinvent your life.

Although some divinatory meanings of this card are thoughtlessness, folly, apathy, frivolity, extravagance, lack of discipline, immaturity, irrationality, hesitation, indecision, delirium, frenzy, enthusiasm and naïvety, it also proclaims that nothing can harm you, whatever you do, so take a risk! It does, however, advise to look before you leap - for a measured, calculated risk will reap the greatest rewards, or lessons. This card symbolises new beginnings in all senses, courageous leaps into some different phase of life, particularly potent when that jump is taken from some inner prompting and deep feeling rather than careful planning. Not limited by ordinary social conventions, and uncomplicated and unanalytical by nature, the Fool is never afraid to believe in something divine or greater than ego. Naturally flowing, trusting, naïve and spontaneous, the Fool often takes a leap into the cosmic experience without fear or expectation. Such is the nature of erratic and unpredictable Uranus.

It is the Fool in each of us which urges us away from lethargy and towards enlightenment and transformation without fear of what's ahead. The Fool is the part of you who, paradoxically, does not worry about being foolish but at the same time, is probably more open to the accusation. He represents the part of ourselves that simply doesn't care what other people think or how things might look. In this way, the Fool enjoys a pure, playful sense of life and a willingness to try new things, regardless of potential consequences or outcomes. In many ways, this card's symbolism can be an agent of awakening and a ripe time for our inner child to emerge.

The Fool is an adventurous card, always ready to change, and is a great significator of luck and possibility, spontaneity, an unknown step forward, the start of a new chapter in life, and a fresh beginning in something. It symbolises throwing caution to the wind and letting it carry you where it will. It suggests that unconventional people will enter your life throughout your travels to share a part of your journey with you, and it also tells you to expect the unexpected at all crossroads. An unexpected influence will soon come into play, such as the possibility of adventure or escape or sudden opportunity. Trust yourself, for even if he is afraid, the Fool is able to win others over with instinctive wit, innocence and kindness, opening up doors and windows for opportunity everywhere he goes. The Universe seems to favour those who are open and willing to be moved and carried along by its flow, and accordingly blesses them with growthful and delightful experiences.

The Fool's number is zero (or unnumbered, like the Joker in a deck of playing cards), the circle, the symbol of eternity, symbolising the ending of the journey back at the beginning, wise and transformed by your travels. It can also be regarded as unnumbered, and has been placed at number 22. The most complex and 'human' of the cards, the Fool, the innocent, the wise man, the trickster, embodying all of humanity's contradictions (male/female, good/evil, angel/devil, etc.), the Fool is a symbol of potentiality and beginnings.

Aquarians, who are influenced by this card through its association with Uranus, could do well to heed its simple messages, keeping them young in spirit, spontaneous, open to life and receptive to opportunities. It would help to identify with the Fool and get in touch with your impractical, illogical and possibly even silly side, and take a leap of faith into the abyss. Trusting that love flows through the

Universe will allow your desires emerge into reality. To really know the Fool is to one's 'inner elf', the eternal, good-humoured prankster that lives just outside the restrictive boundaries of the externally-imposed idea of the self.

When working with this card, ask yourself what you hope to gain from your journey through life, starting from this moment. It is also worth noting and reminding yourself that even a fool can have flashes of great wisdom and sudden lightning bolt thoughts, reminiscent of the brilliant but ever-unpredictable Uranus.

Aquarians are recommended to carry one of these cards with them to illumine their paths, and to magnetise that for which they are asking. Go forth and claim the adventurous horizons which await you by using the symbolism of the Fool as your guide.

★ THE WORLD/UNIVERSE ★

Ruled By Saturn

KEY THEMES

★ Completion ★ Success ★ A Prize or Goal Reached ★
Acclaim ★ Graduation ★ Accomplishment ★ Attainment
★

Meditation ★ "I have completed one journey and will now rebirth myself to begin a brand new one. I welcome every chance to grow and learn."

The World (or Universe), the final card of the Major Arcana, is the supreme symbol of unity and wholeness. It commonly depicts a dancing figure holding the Magician's wand and encircled by a laurel wreath. The wand is symbolic of the magic of self-transformation, while the laurel is the plant of success, victory and high achievement. The circle represents the ouraboros (a serpent or dragon eating its own tail), a symbol of eternity. In each corner are the four fixed signs of the zodiac: Taurus the Bull, Leo the Lion, Scorpio the Eagle and Aquarius the Man, which correspond to the four seasons of spring, summer, autumn and winter respectively, the four evangelical qualities of Man: humanity, spirituality, courage and strength, and also the four elements, which the alchemists combined to create a perfect fifth - the 'quintessence', or fifth element. This fifth element is symbolised by the central figure in the card, a genderless hermaphrodite, an image of the reconciliation of opposites, and also of balance. The card's number is twenty-one, the number of completion (three times seven, the two most magically significant numbers). The wreath may also represent zero, the symbol of infinity, with which you started the journey; therefore, the end of one journey is marking the beginning of another.

The World's divinatory meanings are completion, perfection, the rewards of labour and success, the end result of all your efforts, success, synthesis, fulfilment, capability, eternal life, admiration from others, ultimate change, and triumph in all your undertakings.

Without attachment, the figure in the World image releases the past and dances ecstatically into the future, in an open space and to his or her own rhythm, within a circle of support. The Tarot traveller, at the end of the journey, realises that the individual is the symbol of the whole world, embracing all things within the enlightened self.

This is considered the most auspicious card in the pack, indicating great success, and showing that battles have been fought and won, challenges have been faced, and victory is yours. When the World appears in a reading, it means you have in some sense mastered the three planes of mind, body and emotions, having come to know yourself in a way that makes you feel at home with yourself. You have reached a great balance and integration and are in a place of knowing all parts of yourself and using them for the expression of your real self in the world. As well as triumph, this card also signifies transcendence, and your experience of it may be hard to define or put into rational words. You may just sense and feel that you are elated, spirited and aware, with the new wisdom and insights you've gathered along the way to carry into your next phase.

The World also marks the end of a period of time, the completion of a task, which has its new beginnings as a seed within. It denotes a time of celebration and the wonderful feelings that accompany any occasion during which something is finished, or made whole. It represents a deeply satisfying sense of achievement and fulfilment, suggestive of a peak experience - and expanded horizons ahead. On another level, however, any accomplishment or completion may be followed afterwards by a feeling of emptiness or deflation, as the goal has been realised and the dream made a reality. At this point, the crowned dancing figure who celebrates reaching the finishing mark, suddenly morphs again to embody a foetal-like being, waiting to re-evolve and rebirth itself as the Fool in the never-ending circular journey; in this way, The World symbolises the ending of one cycle and the commencement of another, and indeed The World represents a course that has now come full circle. You now understand your place within that system, and are ready to begin a new phase from the beginning, but this time with an elevated, higher sense of acquired wisdom, spiritual truth and inner knowing.

THE TAROT'S SUIT OF SWORDS - REPRESENTING THE AIR ELEMENT

The Swords correspond with the Air element and are an especially interesting and meaningful metaphor. Swords, or the mind, organise by dividing, and quite literally cutting through things. Air cannot be seen, gripped, grasped or commanded of, and can only be felt with subtle 'other' senses - the higher mind being one of them. We know the air is there through its apparent physical presence such as wisps of wind, but we cannot see it, touch it or even embrace it. In this way, the Swords suit can signify a certain elusiveness, something that can somehow evade us. But it is nonetheless a powerful force. Considered to be powerful and potentially destructive and dangerous, the Tarot Swords can indicate battles and enemies, but they can also be used constructively, to summon courage and a more conscious quality of mind. The Swords may be connected with hostility, struggle, action, change, bitterness, power, oppression, malice and conflict, but they are also associated with fortitude, audacity, strength, bravery, ambition and force, as well as with ideas and communication. Swords are almost always double-edged, which symbolises the fine balance that is needed between the intellect and power, and how these two forces can be used for good or evil. In a deck of playing cards, Swords correspond to Spades.

THE LUCKY 13 ★ AQUARIAN TIPS FOR INCREASED MAGIC, LUCK & MAGNETISM

1. Incorporate Aquarian symbols into your daily life to remind yourself of your soul's mission

2. Use the crystal Amethyst in any form in your daily life - wear it, meditate with it, hold it and carry it with you everywhere!

3. Wear or surround yourself with the colour electric blue and the stone or the colour turquoise. Turquoise is the stone of friendship, and so aligns with the Eleventh House, which is the astrological house ruled by Aquarius. It also brings hope, discovery, peace and balance, all of which are emotions or states of being that assist in attracting wonderful things to you.

4. Learn the way of 'the Lion' by learning courage, boldness and confidence. Leo has much to teach the Aquarian soul. Roar … Wear the crown … Seat yourself at the head of the Table of Life … Feel the wonders of the plains under your feet … Enjoy the feasts and fruits of your journey … Lead the pride … Sit atop the Mighty Throne… it's all within you!

5. Connect with your brilliant ideas through any means possible.

6. Magnify and celebrate your originality, quirks, eccentricities, uniqueness and inventiveness.

7. Remind yourself of your mission constantly, that is by speaking, breathing and *truly living* your brilliant ideas and insights - bring them out into the sunshine!

8. Focus your energies on exploring your inner genius and transforming yourself through your higher thinking faculties - which are strongly accessible to the acutely intellectually-sensitive Aquarian mind.

9. Use your innate power of magnetism and futuristic thinking to visualise and draw that which you desire towards you.

10. Tap into and utilise your ability to guide, heal and transform others through sharing your mind and thoughts. But to do that, you'll need to come down from that lonely mountaintop from time to time. We need you down here!

11. View your eccentric nature as a strength and call forth the powers of your unusual, gifted, unique self. Be who you really are and the rest will fall into place.

12. Become the 'Original Inventor' that you were born to be!

13. Once you have mastered true self-confidence, courage and boldness, learn to share the resulting abundance, insights and knowledge with others!

HAVE YOU PACKED YOUR MAGICAL BAG FOR THE JOURNEY?

If you wish to increase and draw luck, love and abundance into your life, a power pack is essential. For Aquarians, I would recommend carrying or wearing the following items on you on your travels. Then just sit back and watch as magic pours into your experiences and realities, both inner and outer!

★ One of each of the following gemstones: Turquoise, Garnet, Aquamarine, Amethyst, Zircon

★ Tarot Cards The Star and The Fool (and The World/Universe card too, if you wish)

★ An otter in any form (use your imagination!)

★ Something made of lead

★ A Key symbol in any form

★ A postcard or image from a tropical place (representing your Sanguine disposition) Bon Voyage!

★ A postcard from the future to yourself, proclaiming, 'Wish You Were Here!'

A FINAL WORD ★ TAPPING INTO THE MAGIC OF AQUARIUS

There is something inherently magical about Aquarius, the Water Bearer. Blessed with a lack of arrogance, a brilliant mind and dazzling foresight, they truly are the Magical Future-Dwellers of the zodiac, affecting everyone around them with their power and sense of the weird and wonderful. Never malicious but ever perversely contradictory and rebellious, the Aquarian soul wants to connect with other like-minded souls. To really tap into your true magic, this mind and soul connection with kindred spirits is imperative to your life's spring of wellbeing. You are the sign of the group leader. Connect! Exchange! Brainstorm! Share! Embrace! Love! Shine!

Inside anyone who has a strong Aquarius influence in their natal chart, is someone who is deeply uncertain of their identity. The typical Aquarian possesses a powerful and magnetic intellect, but your ego is said to be the weakest and most precarious of the zodiac; you are not a proficient self-promoter and generally shy away from attention and focus. Although perversely reluctant to share your sparkling ideas, talent and futuristic prophecies, Aquarius is often under-credited and is actually the most intellectual of the signs; underneath a cool façade, you are pure genius just bursting with mind-blowing ideas that need to be brought out to air! They're no use sitting in the dusty recesses of your mind ... or off wildly living it up on some other planet.

Further, like your ruling planet Uranus, you are the Divine Rebel of the zodiac, and although this can pay dividends in the form of societal change, you need to build within yourself a strong centre that you can return to in order to rest and refresh. Aquarius rules the circulatory system, and while this assists in the movement of your thoughts, you also need that strong centre to fall back on; for this, you would do well to take lessons in *heart* from your opposite sign, Leo, and its rulership over the heart, the life force, the core, *the centre*. Your mind and nervous system usually rule you, rather than the other way around. In order to master yourself, you need to put yourself in a position to manifest on the earthly plane that which you visualise by becoming one with the source of your mind. This means you have to find a way to observe your own prodigious thinking processes and not just *be* your thoughts - by keeping them cooped up and creating nervous system and minor mental health disturbances in the process, which is at the root of your suffering.

There is tremendous creative and visionary potential inherent in Aquarius, but you are also fixed and tenacious, meaning that may have difficulties giving up old opinions, ideas and positions that should've been left behind long ago. While you're busy living in the future, the ideas of your past may be stuck on that stick in the stream. Unpack your baggage from time to time, Aquarius, the journey is a lot lighter without it!

Ultimately, your sign represents freedom, especially the kind of freedom which comes from transcending the body and earthly life, freedom of thought, the power of individuality harnessed to serve the greater whole, and importantly (to Aquarians at least) the union of science and magic. Aquarians are big believers in magic, despite everything their logical left brain has 'taught' them. Not only can they get completely lost in Wonderland, they believe wholeheartedly in the adage, "When in Rome (or Wonderland) …" - they just do it a little differently to the Wonderlandians in order to stand out - and will live by this motto their entire lives. Which isn't a bad thing at all. The world needs more souls of your ilk, who stand apart from the herd. Great things transpire from those who dare to be different and above all, from those who dare to dream.

Finally, to attune yourself to luck, harmony and success, Aquarians should wear, eat, inhale, meditate upon, create, design, and dance with any or all of the suggested power-enhancers for your Sun sign to receive the most beneficial astral vibrations these 'boosters' can offer you.

I sincerely wish you all the luck, energy, love, abundance, happiness and personal power you can muster through working with the magical energies outlined throughout *Power Astrology: Aquarius*. This book has been written with your Sun sign's energies and interests at heart, and with my unwavering faith that you can - and indeed will be - expanded, blessed, charmed and luckier should you put them to the test. Cosmic strokes of luck will soon rain down upon you just for having read this book, and I hope it has made you grow in some way. This, my fellow Aquarian friends, I promise you, because I too am an Aquarian and *I know* - and Aquarians, being the eternal truth-seekers, *never* lie.

Good luck on the rest of your amazing life journey, and may the POWER be with you!

☆

"She's susceptible to sudden flashes of inspiration, and her intuition is remarkable. Her judgement may not seem sound or practical at first, because she sees months and years ahead.

The Aquarian girl lives in tomorrow. What she says will come true, perhaps after many delays and troubles, but it will come true.

I suppose, after all, that's the most special thing about your Aquarian woman. She's a little big magic."

♒

Linda Goodman

www.ingramcontent.com/pod-product-compliance
Lightning Source LLC
Chambersburg PA
CBHW071917290426
44110CB00013B/1392